MASTERING UNREAL ENGINE 5

From

BEGINNER TO PRO

The Definitive Guide to Building High-Quality Games, Immersive Virtual Worlds, and Advanced Interactive Contents

Kai J. Tempest

Mastering Unreal Engine 5 from Beginner to Pro: The Definitive Guide to Building High-Quality Games, Immersive Virtual Worlds, and Advanced Interactive Contents.

First edition. April 2025.

Written by Kai J. Tempest

Contents

Chapter 1

Getting Started with Unreal Engine

Introduction to the Unreal Engine (UE)

Unreal Engine (alternatively called UE) is quite possibly one of the most advanced, versatile, and utilized game engines in the world. Developed by Epic Games, it evolved from a simple utility program for creating first-person shooters to a stable platform that can support not just games but movies, architectural visualizations, simulations, and virtual reality activities as well. With its innovative graphics, high-performance feature, and vast toolset, Unreal Engine is now the top preference for numerous developers, artists, and companies in various industries.

Unreal Engine is the leader in the pack due to its massive-scale features and attributes, enabling programmers to create amazing, engaging applications across a number of industry verticals. Some of its fundamental capabilities include high-end graphics, render capability, and real-world illumination. Features such as Nanite, Lumen, ray tracing, and PBR enable programmers to have high-end visuals with unbelievable details and realism.

One of the most user-friendly UE features is its Blueprint visual scripting system, under which developers can create complex game logic without writing any code. This node-based system makes it easier for artists and designers to implement mechanics, AI behaviors, and interactions, releasing them from dependence on programmers.

Unreal Engine can handle development on a wide range of platforms, including PC, consoles (PlayStation, Xbox, Nintendo Switch), mobile (iOS, Android), virtual reality (VR), and augmented reality (AR). The cross-platform support means that developers can create games and apps for many different ecosystems easily.

With physics engines like Chaos included within the framework and AI capabilities like behavior trees and navigation meshes, UE allows developers to create extremely interactive and intelligent worlds. From human character animation to destructible terrain, these capabilities increase realism and degree of immersion in digital experiences.

Epic Games unveiled MetaHuman Creator, a powerful software for crafting highly realistic human characters, thankfully, unreal engine makes creating realistic animations and facial expressions convenient with sophisticated animation systems like Control Rig and the integration of motion capture.

In contrast to the majority of proprietary engines, UE opens up its full source code, enabling developers to add and modify the functionality of the engine as per their needs. Such openness fosters a healthy and committed community of developers who go on to enhance the engine further.

Unreal Engine is a gaming giant, but its applications don't end there. The movie business, architecture, automotive, and medical industries are leveraging UE's powerful toolset to revolutionize their workflow. Hollywood movie studios and animation houses have embraced Unreal Engine for real-time rendering and virtual production. Movies such as The Mandalorian have utilized UE's virtual sets to build amazing environments, reducing the number of green-screen rigs required.

Architects and designers utilize Unreal Engine to create interactive 3D models of buildings and environments. Through real-time rendering, clients can view properties in realistic virtual reality even before they are built, optimizing design visualization and decision-making.

Car makers utilize Unreal Engine for virtual prototyping, car testing, and marketing presentation. UE's highly realistic car model rendering allows designers to refine their designs and show their products in a very compelling manner.

The healthcare industry is benefited by Unreal Engine's simulation capability, which enables healthcare professionals to practice surgeries, diagnose patients, and train in virtual environments that mimic real-world conditions without any actual risk. With virtual learning and business training simulations on the rise, Unreal Engine provides an immersive platform for educators and trainers to design interactive learning spaces, ranging from VR history to complex engineering simulations.

Unreal Engine also finds growing application in the military and defense sectors, where it is used to design training simulations, battlefield visualizations, and mission planning systems. Its ability for hyper-realistic environment production allows soldiers to be trained in virtual settings that accurately represent real-world settings.

In product design and manufacture, Unreal Engine is used to conduct digital prototyping, with savings in time and cost. Engineers and designers get to experience and improve upon their products using a virtual model prior to a final decision of manufacture.

Another major advantage of Unreal Engine is its marketplace and community. Epic Games has designed a strong ecosystem through which developers can trade assets, tools, and plugins on the Unreal Marketplace. This reduces time in development and enables creators to focus on innovation rather than re-inventing solutions that already exist.

Unreal Engine's artificial intelligence (AI) and machine learning capabilities are also increasing, allowing for more advanced non-player character (NPC) actions, procedural generation of content, and game design automation. AI-driven software is making it easier to generate realistic animations, voice generation, and dynamic game mechanics.

In addition, Unreal Engine is also a dominant force in metaverse and digital twin technologies. Companies are leveraging UE to create virtual spaces that replicate real spaces so that firms can conduct simulations, digital shopping, and remote collaboration in very immersive settings.

The ease of use of Unreal Engine has vastly increased with simple-to-use tools, rich documentation, and loads of tutorials floating around the net. From newbies to industry veterans, Unreal Engine offers an ecosystem where both creativity and technical skills can find expression.

Its unparalleled graphics potential, simple tools, and sheer versatility in several industries make Unreal Engine the epicenter of digital innovation for decades to come.

The Importance of Unreal Engine in the Modern Development Environment

Unreal Engine (UE) has become a cornerstone in the modern development environment, below are the reasons why the Unreal Engine is an important part of the modern development environment.

- **Realism and Advanced Graphics:** One of the most striking features of Unreal Engine is the ability to render high-quality graphics. UE leverages powerful rendering techniques, including real-time ray tracing, to deliver realistic lighting and shadows. This aspect is important for game designers and filmmakers who want to offer compelling experiences. The level of graphics fidelity that UE supports allows creators to break new ground in terms of realism and surprise audiences with stunning visuals.

- **Flexible Game Development**: Unreal Engine is used to develop games of every genre, from action and adventure to simulation and role-playing games. Its features and tools are scalable to small independent projects and even huge AAA games. UE permits developers to take advantage of its blueprint system, a visual scripting system that simplifies the process of coding. This is easier for new developers to break into game development, allowing a new generation of game developers.

- **Support for Multiple Platforms**: UE provides support for many platforms, ranging from PC, consoles, mobiles, and VR systems. The support provides a platform through which developers are able to build games that gain more exposure. With one codebase, the developers are able to deploy on multiple platforms with minimal changes. This saves resources and time and is a convenient option for developers seeking extensive penetration into the market.

- **Bigger Community and Resources:** The UE community is large and active. There are plenty of resources for developers to utilize, including tutorials, forums, and documentation. Epic Games, the creator of UE, updates the engine constantly and provides support through their community centers. The ecosystem encourages collaboration and allows for quick problem-solving among developers. Collective knowledge borrowed from a massive pool hastens the learning process, especially for new developers of games.

- **Integration With Cutting-Edge Technology:** Unreal Engine is also at the forefront of technology integration. It is able to support emerging trends such as VR and AR. The engine can be used to create rich, immersive experiences that are not just restricted to games. UE is also being used in sectors such as architecture and medicine to perform simulations and training, offering higher realism in their presentation materials and training tools.

- **Collaboration and Interoperability:** Unreal Engine promotes the collaboration of developers, artists, and designers. Unreal Engine tools support interoperability with other software applications such as Maya, Blender, and Photoshop. Using tools allows collaborative work teams to accomplish this together, more effectively. Exporting and importing assets is not a significant problem, making multidisciplinary collaboration easier.

- **Marketplace and Asset Store:** The Unreal Engine Marketplace offers an assortment of assets, including 3D models, audio, and plugins. Developers can sell or purchase assets, and this accelerates the process of project development. The marketplace fosters innovation and enables developers to find the resources needed to enhance their projects. Through lessening the obstacle of getting high-quality assets, UE empowers developers to focus on creativity rather than starting from the beginning.

- **Industry Adoption:** UE has also gained popularity beyond gaming. It is used by filmmakers for virtual production, allowing them to visualize scenes in real-time.

Architectural firms employ UE for walkthroughs and presentations, showing clients designs with stunning realism. This cross-industry application demonstrates the flexibility and versatility of UE. It shows how the engine can be a powerful tool beyond its original gaming purpose.

- **Constant Updates and Innovation:** Epic Games focuses on keeping Unreal Engine current with technology. Regular updates introduce new features and improvements, enabling developers to leverage the latest innovations. The updates typically result from feedback from the community, which allows the engine to evolve according to how its users require it. Staying current with trends enables developers to create relevant and engaging content.

- **Cost-Effectiveness:** Unreal Engine is on a royalty model. Developers can download and use UE for free until their game or project makes a lot of money. That makes the initial entry barrier low, open to indie developers and small studios. It allows them to experiment and innovate without having to pay large amounts of money up front, resulting in creativity and diversity in game development.

- **Learning and Educational Resources:** The majority of learning schools currently incorporate Unreal Engine in their curriculum. Emphasis on education around UE equips students with work-applicable skills. UE learning gives students an advantage in employment competition as the engine is familiar to the profession. Workshops, tutorials, and courses are now readily available and enable students to learn skills in game design and others with greater ease.

- **Empowering Creativity:** At its essence, Unreal Engine enables creativity. The features and tools enable developers to bring their visions to life without restriction. Whether developing a compelling game world or creating a complex film scene, UE offers the platform to make ideas a reality. This embracing of creativity fuels innovation and extends boundaries in all digital media.

Current Industry Applications of the Unreal Engine- Gaming, Film, Architecture, etc.

Unreal Engine (UE), developed by Epic Games, has expanded far beyond its initial role as a game engine. Its powerful real-time rendering, high-definition graphics, and versatility have made it an essential tool in many industries. From gaming and filmmaking to architecture and even the medical field, Unreal Engine is revolutionizing the creation and consumption of digital content. Below, are five of the largest industry applications of Unreal Engine:

- **Gaming Industry**: Gaming is where Unreal Engine began, and it remains one of its main uses. The engine offers advanced graphics, top-notch performance, and robust tools with which developers can build engaging and visually appealing games. A few of the most important ways Unreal Engine is utilized within gaming are:

1. **Real-Time Rendering**: Unreal Engine's real-time rendering feature makes it possible for developers to view changes in real-time, making the game development process more efficient.

2. **Photorealistic Graphics**: Strong lighting, textures, and shading techniques help creators construct realistic game worlds.

3. **Multiplatform Support**: UE supports different platforms like PC, consoles, mobile, and VR/AR headsets for maximum reach.

4. **Blueprint Visual Scripting**: The feature allows creators, even those who don't know long codes, to easily construct complex game mechanics.

5. **Advanced AI and Physics:** The engine includes AI assets that help with intelligent NPC behavior and natural physics simulations for more immersive gameplay.

It is important to note: Fortnite, Gears of War, Final Fantasy VII Remake, and Valorant are a few of the most popular games built using Unreal Engine.

- **Film and Television Production:** The film and television production sector has embraced Unreal Engine en masse for applications in all areas of production, particularly virtual production and visual effects (VFX). Major studios are leveraging UE to revolutionize filmmaking with the following applications:

    1. **Virtual Production**: Filmmakers can create virtual sets and locations that actors can improvise from in real-time, reducing the need for much physical set building.

    2. **Previsualization (Previs)**: Directors and cinematographers get to see scenes in advance prior to cameras beginning to roll, improving planning and efficiency.

    3. **Real-Time Rendering for VFX**: Long rendering time is usually prevalent with conventional VFX pipelines, but Unreal Engine facilitates real-time rendering, eliminating much post-production lag.

    4. **Character Animation and Motion Capture**: The engine has support for motion capture technology, which allows one to create realistic digital characters.

    5. **LED Volume Technology**: Films like The Mandalorian use Unreal Engine-powered LED screens to create dynamic backgrounds, replacing green screens with real-time digital environments.

- **Architecture and Real Estate:** Unreal Engine has been a game-changer in architecture, engineering, and construction (AEC) fields. It allows architects and designers to create real-time visualizations of buildings and spaces, which helps in better communication with clients and stakeholders. Some of the major uses are:

    1. **Real-Time Architectural Visualization**: Architects can create highly detailed, interactive 3D building models and interiors that can be explored by clients in real-time.

2. **Virtual Reality (VR) Walkthroughs:** Potential purchasers and investors are able to view properties before they are built, improving the purchasing process and reducing design miscommunications.

3. **Photorealistic Rendering:** UE enables highly realistic lighting, materials, and textures, which create digital representations almost indistinguishable from real buildings.

4. **Urban Planning and Smart Cities:** Planners and governments use Unreal Engine to model cityscapes, allowing for better planning and infrastructure development.

5. **Interactive Design Modifications:** Designers can alter architectural models in real-time, observing changes to lighting, materials, and structure in real-time.

- **Automotive and Manufacturing:** The automotive and manufacturing industries are increasingly using Unreal Engine for design visualization, training, and even marketing. The ability to create high-fidelity, real-time simulations has led to several revolutionary uses, including:

  1. **Car Design and Prototyping**: Automakers use Unreal Engine to create digital copies of vehicles, allowing real-time modification and design changes before actual physical models are constructed.

  2. **Virtual Showrooms**: Audi, BMW, and Tesla are among companies that use UE to create interactive virtual showrooms where clients can customize and see cars in depth.

  3. **Simulations for Driver Training**: Unreal Engine is being applied in driving simulators to educate commercial drivers, test autonomous vehicle systems, and refine safety training.

  4. **Factory and Assembly Line Design**: Manufacturers are able to model production lines in Unreal Engine, optimizing workflows and identifying areas where inefficiency may be possible before actual changes are made in the physical world.

  5. **Marketing and Advertising**: UE's high-quality 3D graphics and animation allow automobile manufacturers to produce compelling adverts and marketing literature without the need for actual physical prototypes.

- **Healthcare and Medical Training:** The healthcare industry has started leveraging Unreal Engine for medical training, surgical simulation, and patient education. The ability to create interactive and very real medical environments provides UE an advantage in the healthcare industry. Its major uses include:

1. **Surgical Simulations:** Through Unreal Engine, medical professionals and students can practice surgical procedures in a virtual environment, reducing chances of actual training.

2. **Medical Visualization**: Doctors use UE to create 3D visualizations of the human form to aid in planning complex surgeries and explaining intricate procedures to patients.

3. **VR-Based Medical Training:** VR training sessions enabled by Unreal Engine are used by medical schools to train students and professionals in emergency response scenarios, anatomy, and diagnosis.

4. **Therapeutic Applications:** VR experiences enabled by Unreal Engine are used for pain control, exposure therapy, and rehabilitation therapy.

5. **Patient Education**: Patients are able to learn about conditions and treatments using interactive simulations, improving doctor-patient communication.

Chapter 2

Features and Specifications of the Unreal Engine

Nanite (Virtualized Geometry)

One of the most innovative features in Unreal Engine 5 is Nanite. It is a virtualized geometry system that allows developers to use film-quality assets with billions of polygons without compromising real-time performance. In contrast to traditional rendering methods that employ level-of-detail (LOD) techniques to gain performance, Nanite streams and optimizes geometry on the automatically without any noticeable decrease in visual fidelity.

How Does Nanite Works?

1. **Virtualized Micropolygon Geometry**: Nanite only loads and renders triangles as required, based on what's visible to the camera, to prevent performance issues due to large polygon counts.

2. **Automatic Level of Details (LOD) Generation:** Instead of manually creating multiple LODs for an asset, Nanite dynamically adapts the level of detail in response to the distance from the viewer.

3. **Efficient Memory Usage**: With its data compression and streaming technology integrated, Nanite minimizes memory footprint without a loss of fidelity.

4. **Tight Integration With Other UE5 Features:** Nanite is coupled with Lumen for global illumination, ray tracing, and high-quality texture streaming.

Quick Step-By-Step Guide to Using Nanite in Unreal Engine 5

1. Enable Nanite in Your Project:

   o Launch Unreal Engine 5 and create a new project or open an existing project.

   o Navigate to **Project Settings > Rendering** and ensure that **Nanite** is enabled.

   o Restart Unreal Engine for the changes to be applied.

2. Import High-Resolution Assets:

   o Open **Content Browser**, click **Import** to import high-poly assets (e.g., ZBrush sculpts, CAD models, or photogrammetry assets).

o   Unreal Engine will automatically convert these assets to Nanite-compatible geometry.

3.   Enable Nanite on an Asset:

o   Select the imported mesh and open the **Static Mesh Editor**.

o   In the **Details** panel, toggle on the **Nanite Enabled** option.

o   Click **Apply Changes**, and the asset will now be utilizing Nanite's virtualized geometry system.

4.   Adjust Performance with Nanite Settings:

o   Modify **Triangle Budget** to control memory consumption.

o   Use **Screen Size Scaling** to adjust LOD transitions.

o   Enable **Nanite Debug View** in the **viewport t**o visualize how the engine is rendering polygons.

5.   Real-Time Test and Adjustments:

o   Put the Nanite-enabled assets in your level.

o   Utilize the Unreal Engine's **FPS Counter and GPU Profiler** to track performance.

o   Alter the settings to suit your platform's target performance (e.g., PC, console, VR).

How to Apply Nanite

1.   **Game Development:** Enables high-detail environments without a performance loss.

2.   **Film Production**: Allows the utilization of movie-quality assets for real-time rendering.

3.   **Architecture & Automotive**: Manages complex CAD models without manual optimization.

4.   **Virtual Reality (VR):** Reduces draw calls without a loss of detail for an immersive experience.

Lumen (Real-Time Global Illumination)

This is a powerful illumination system within Unreal Engine. It aids with a lighting mechanism that reacts to changes in the environment. Unlike traditional lighting techniques, Lumen eliminates pre-baked lighting. It brings realism and efficiency to rendering.

What Are the Benefits of Lumen?

Lumen is built to manage complicated light situations in real time. It replicates the way light interacts with objects and surfaces. The outcome is practical shadows, reflections, and indirect lighting. Some of its key advantages are:

1. **Dynamic Lighting**: Lighting changes are reflected immediately.
2. **Realistic Reflections**: Accurate reflections of surroundings on surfaces.
3. **Efficient Workflow**: No time-consuming light baking required.
4. **Scalability:** Performs on different hardware setups.

Quick Steps to Set Up the Lumen in Unreal Engine

1. Activate Lumen:
   - Open Unreal Engine and start a new project.
   - Go to Edit > Project Settings.
   - Open Rendering.
   - Under Global Illumination, choose **Lumen**.
   - Make sure Reflection Method is also **Lumen**.
   - Restart the engine to enable changes.
2. Modify Lumen Quality Settings:
   - Launch the **Post Process Volume** in the scene.
   - Navigate to find Global Illumination Method.
   - Change it to **Lumen.**
   - Change **Lumen Scene Detail** for higher quality.
   - Change **Final Gather Quality** to adjust noise and detail.
3. Adjust and Improve Performance:
   - Lower **Lumen Scene Detail** for lower-end hardware.
   - Reduce **Software Ray Tracing Quality** if performance drops.
   - Use **Hardware Ray Tracing** on high-end GPUs.
   - Enable **Screen Traces** to improve efficiency.

What Are the Key Functions of Lumen?

Lumen offers various functions that improve lighting realism, and they include:

1. Real-Time Global Illumination:

    - Light bounces off surfaces dynamically.

    - Changes in lighting affect the entire scene instantly.

    - Enhances indoor and outdoor lighting realism.

2. Indirect Lighting:

    - Light reflects off walls and objects.

    - Dark areas receive natural illumination.

    - Eliminates the need for static lightmaps.

3. Diffuse Interreflection:

    - Softens harsh light transitions.

    - Increases material realism.

    - Suitable for interiors and exteriors.

4. Dynamic Reflections:

    - It causes reflection to Water, glass, and metal surface.

    - Changes with camera movement and light.

    - Provides realism in outdoor scenes and gameplay.

When to Use the Lumen?

Lumen is used in various scenarios, because it increases visual standard and reduces workflows. You can use Lumen in the following scenarios:

1. Game Development:

    - It creates a realistic lighting environment.

    - Allows for day-night cycles without pre-baked lighting.

    - Provides realism in open-world and indoor scenes.

2. Film and Virtual Production:

    - It obviates the need for expensive lighting setups.

    - It activates real-time visualization for changes in lightening.

    - You can use it in LED volume stages for dynamic backgrounds.

3. Architectural Visualization:

- It provides realistic lighting for buildings and interiors.
- Enables real-time modifications to light positions.
- It assists clients to envisage designs more precisely.

4. Automotive and Product Design:
   - It provides correct reflections on the surfaces of cars
   - It assists to visualize materials and lighting conditions.
   - It obviates the need for high-end rendering software.

Metasounds (Advanced Audio System)

This is a high-level procedural audio system in Unreal Engine. It provides high-level control over sound generation and sound processing. Unlike traditional sound systems, MetaSounds is a modular approach to audio design. It allows for audio manipulation and is viable for games, virtual production, and interactive applications.

MetaSounds is designed for dynamic, high-quality sound generation. It's based on a node-based system that allows for real-time audio synthesis and manipulation. Some of the key benefits include:

1. **Audio Processing**: Sound changes dynamically in reaction to in-game activity.
2. **Modular Sound Design**: It allows users to create complex audio without the need for external software.
3. **Improved Performance: It** enhances performance on a range of hardware platforms.
4. **Scalability:** It can be used on both simple sound effects and complex music compositions.

How to Quickly Setup the MetaSounds in Unreal Engine

To use MetaSounds, follow these steps:

1. Enable MetaSounds:
   o Launch Unreal Engine and start a new project.
   o Go to Edit > Plugins.
   o Navigate and click on **MetaSounds,** to enable it.
   o Restart the engine for changes to take effect.
2. Create a MetaSound Source:
   o Right-click in the Content Browser.

o   Choose Sounds > MetaSound Source.

o   Launch the MetaSound Editor.

o   Insert nodes to create a custom sound network.

3.   Integrate MetaSound into a Scene:

o   Drag the MetaSound Source into the level.

o   Add it to an Audio Component.

o   Modify options like pitch, volume, and filters.

Features of MetaSounds

MetaSounds provides advanced features that enhance audio design and interactivity. Some of its features include:

1.   Procedural Audio Generation:

o   Create real-time synthesized sounds.

o   Dynamically alter sounds based on player actions.

o   Utilize oscillators, envelopes, and filters for bespoke audio.

2.   Modular Node System:

o   Combine various nodes to synthesize distinctive sounds.

o   Quickly alter parameters without external software.

o   Reuse sound graphs for various effects.

3.   Parameter-Driven Audio:

o   Control sound behavior with real-time parameters.

o   Adjust volume, pitch, and frequency based on in-game events.

o   Connect sound changes to animations and physics interactions.

4.   Spatialized and 3D Audio:

o   Simulate real-world acoustics.

o   Produce immersive audio environments.

o   Adjust sound properties based on object positions.

How to Use/Apply MetaSounds

MetaSounds is used in a wide range of applications, from gaming to interactive media:

1. Game Audio Design:
   - Generate unique sound effects dynamically.
   - Bind audio changes to player interactions.
   - Increase immersion with real-time sound manipulation.

2. Virtual Production:
   - Enhance real-time filmmaking with dynamic sound.
   - Edit sound based on camera angles and scenes.
   - Maximize post-production sound editing time.

3. Architectural Visualization:
   - Simulate environmental audio from the real world.
   - Adjust reverb and reflections based on room size.
   - Create a better experience for clients and designers.

4. Automotive and Product Design:
   - Create interactive soundscapes for car simulations.
   - Design sound feedback for mechanical and UI interactions.
   - Enhance marketing presentations with real-time sound.

World Partition & One File Per Actor (Large Open-World Development)

World Partition and One File Per Actor (OFPA) are two critical Unreal Engine features that significantly improve large open-world development. They allow developers to create massive, seamless worlds while optimizing performance and collaborative workflows.

World Partition is an alternative to the traditional level streaming system in Unreal Engine and offers a more scalable and automated way of dealing with large worlds. It allows for enormous environments to be divided into a grid and loaded or unloaded dynamically based on player proximity, with a huge improvement in performance.

Features of World Partition

1. **Grid-Based Streaming**: Instead of setting up level streaming volumes, world partitioning automatically handles world streaming by dividing the landscape into a grid.

2. **Automatic Loading and Unloading:** Grid cells only load as and when needed, conserving memory and improving performance.

3. **Hierarchical Level of Detail (HLOD):** Automatic simplification of distant areas is allowed, reducing rendering load.

4. **Collaborative Editing:** Multiple developers can be editing different parts of the same world at the same time without getting in each other's way.

5. **Smooth Transitions:** Offers seamless streaming between parts of the world without noticeable loading screens.

Using the World Partition

1. **Activate World Partition**: When starting a new level, select the option for World Partition.

2. **Migrate Current Levels**: Current levels can be migrated using Unreal's conversion tools.

3. **Set Up Streaming Priorities**: Use **Data Layers** and **HLOD** settings to stream the world efficiently and render it.

4. **Optimize and Test**: Use profiling tools to ensure that the assets stream in perfectly and performance is smooth.

One File Per Actor (OFPA) Vis-À-Vis Streamlined Collaboration

One File Per Actor allows Unreal Engine to store each actor in its own file instead of bundling all content into a single level file. This fundamentally improves version control and collaboration for large teams.

The Importance of One File Per Actor

1. **Improved Source Control**: Developers can modify different actors without causing merge conflicts.

2. **Faster Modification**: Modifications to an actor do not require saving the entire level.

3. **Efficient Asset Management**: Easier tracking of changes and troubleshooting.

4. **Improved Loading**: Only changed actors need to be loaded, improving workflow efficiency.

Using the One File Per Actor

1. Enable (One File Per Actor) OFPA: In the project settings, enable "One File Per Actor".

2. **Save Actors Separately**: When modifying actors, changes are stored in their individual files.

3. **Use With Source Control**: Apply Git, Perforce, or SVN to track and manage actor modifications efficiently.

4. **Improve Workflow:** Assign different actors to team members to improve parallel development.

Chaos Physics & Destruction

Chaos Physics is Unreal Engine's high-performance physics and destruction system, designed to provide state-of-the-art real-time simulation of physics-based interactions. It is an important tool for creating destructible environments, realistic object behavior, and dynamic world interactions in games and simulations.

Features of Chaos Physics

1. **Rigid Body Dynamics**: Physically simulates interaction between objects in a realistic manner, allowing for realistic motion and collision.

2. **Destruction System**: Enables real-time fracturing and breaking of objects, essential for destruction gameplay.

3. **Cloth and Soft Body Physics**: Physically simulates the behavior of fabrics, soft substances, and deformable surfaces.

4. **Vehicle Physics:** Provides a sophisticated system for simulating cars, trucks, and other vehicles with realistic suspension and motion.

5. **Fluid and Particle Simulation**: Can control actual water, dust, and smoke effects for realistic environments.

6. **Physics Constraints**: Allows objects to be attached and move relative to one another, useful for hinges, ropes, and machinery.

How to Use Chaos Physics & Destruction in Unreal Engine

- Enabling Chaos Physics:
    1. Go to Edit > Plugins and enable Chaos Physics.
    2. Restart Unreal Engine for the changes to be applied.
- Creating Destructible Objects:
    1. Insert a **3D model** into Unreal Engine.
    2. Right-click and **Create Geometry Collection** to turn it into a Geometry Collection.
    3. Use the **Fracture tool** to break the object into multiple pieces.

4. Create a damage thresholds and constraints to control destruction behavior.

- Chaos on Rigid Bodies:
    1. Insert a **Static Mesh** to a scene and turn it into a **Physics Actor.**
    2. Check/Click Simulate Physics in the Details panel.
    3. Modify properties such as mass, friction, and bounce.

- Setting Up Vehicle Physics:
    1. Insert a **Vehicle Model** and set up **Wheeled Vehicle** components.
    2. Define tire friction, engine torque, and suspension characteristics.
    3. Add acceleration, brake, and steering controls.

- Simulating Soft Bodies and Cloth:
    1. Add a **Cloth Modifier** to a character's apparel or to a flag.
    2. Create cloth constraints for realistic motion and wind response.

- Tips to Improve Performance:
    1. Apply the **Level of Detail (LOD)** settings to balance performance and visual fidelity.
    2. Activate **GPU** acceleration for physics processing.
    3. Use the Unreal Engine Chaos in-built Debugging tools to profile performance.

Niagara VFX & Control Rig for Animation

The Niagara VFX and Control Rig are powerful tools. They allow users to create detailed visual effects and improve character animation workflows. These tools offer actual changes, making them great tools for game development, filmmaking, and interactive experiences.

Niagara VFX

This is a visual effects system used in Unreal Engine. It is a substitution of the older Cascade system with a new and more capable system. It is used for creating particles, simulations, and dynamic effects.

What Are the Features of Niagara VFX?

1. **Node-Based Editor:** A visual scripting system for effect creation.
2. **GPU Acceleration**: Gives enhanced performance for large effects.
3. **Scalability**: Works with diverse hardware configurations.

4. **Dynamic Particle Behavior**: Allows real-time interaction and physics-based effects.

What Are the Functions of Niagara VFX?

1. **Particle Effects Creation**: It causes smoke, fire, explosions, and magic effects.
2. **Fluid and Gas Simulations**: Creates realistic water, fog, and atmospheric effects.
3. **Advanced Physics-Based Interactions:** Brings environmental and gameplay elements closer to reality.
4. It allows developers to make adjustments to effects without reloading assets.

How to Set Up Niagara VFX

To use Niagara, follow these steps:

Step 1: Enable Niagara in Unreal Engine:

1. Launch Unreal Engine and create a new project.
2. Navigate to Edit > Plugins.
3. Navigate and locate **Niagara** and enable it.
4. Reboot the engine to save changes.

Step 2: Create a Niagara System:

1. Launch the Content Browser.
2. Right-click and navigate to **FX > Niagara System.**
3. Choose a template or an empty system.
4. Launch the **Niagara Editor** and start inserting emitters.

Step 3: Edit Niagara Parameters:

1. Adjust particle size, velocity, and lifespan.
2. Include force fields and collision effects.
3. Utilize shaders for enhanced visuals.

Control Rig

Control Rig is a character rigging tool in Unreal Engine. It enables rea manipulation of animations and movements without external software.

Control Rig Features:

1. **Node-Based Rigging System**: It makes complex animations simpler.
2. **Adjustments**: It allows for instant adjustment of character poses.
3. **Inverse Kinematics (IK) & Forward Kinematics (FK)**: Gives precise control over movement.
4. **Integration With Sequencer**: It enables cinematic and cutscene animation.

Functions of the Control Rig

1. **Character Rigging**: Users can build custom rigs within Unreal Engine.
2. **Motion Capture Integration**: Real-time animation with the help of mocap data.
3. **Pose Manipulation:** Users can make character movement modifications by animators effortlessly.
4. **Animation Layering**: Mix various movements together to create smooth transitions.

How to Set Up the Control Rig

To take advantage of Control Rig, here is what you should do:

Step 1: Activate the Control Rig:

1. Launch Unreal Engine and start a new project.
2. Proceed to Edit > Plugins.
3. Navigate to **Control Rig** and activate it.
4. Restart the engine to activate the changes.

Step 2: Define the Control Rig:

1. Launch the Content Browser.
2. Right-click and choose Animation > Control Rig.
3. Attach a skeletal mesh to the rig.
4. Launch the Control Rig Editor and add controls.

Step 3: Modify the Control Rig Settings:

1. Add **IK** and **FK** solvers for movement control.
2. Insert custom controls for facial expressions.
3. Utilize animation blueprints for refining movements.

4. Use the **Sequencer** to test the rig.

Using the Niagara VFX and Control Rig Jointly

These tools have widespread use in industries. They improve the visual and animation quality of projects.

- Game Development:
    1. **Niagara:** Creates interactive particle effects like fire, water, and explosions.
    2. **Control Rig**: Improves character animation without external tools.
    3. **Combined Use:** Enhances in-game cinematics and cutscenes.
- Film and Virtual Production:
    1. **Niagara:** Creates real-time environmental effects like fog and rain.
    2. **Control Rig**: Animates digital characters with ease.
    3. **Combined Use**: Provides automatic animation feedback to directors and animators.
- Architectural Visualization:
    1. **Niagara:** Adds realistic effects like dust and light reflections.
    2. **Control Rig**: Animates parts that move like doors and elevators.
    3. **Combined Use:** Enriches interactive 3D walkthroughs.
- Automotive and Product Design:
    1. **Niagara:** Creates visual effects for car simulations and motion blur.
    2. **Control Rig:** Animates mechanical parts for demos.
    3. **Combined Use:** Improves marketing presentations and simulations.

Chapter 3

Setting Up Unreal Engine for Development

Unreal Engine 2025 System Requirements

As Unreal Engine continues to evolve, so do its hardware requirements to support advanced features like Nanite, Lumen, Chaos Physics, and real-time ray tracing. Unreal Engine 2025 requires high computational power, especially for developers working on AAA games, virtual production, and large-scale simulations.

Basic System Requirements:

1. **Processor**: Intel Core i7 (10th Gen) or AMD Ryzen 7 (4000 Series)
2. **Internet Connection**: Required for initial installation and updates
3. **Storage**: 500GB SSD (Recommended NVMe)
4. **Operating System:** Windows 10 (64-bit) or macOS (latest version)
5. **RAM:** 16GB DDR4
6. **Graphics Card**: NVIDIA GeForce RTX 3060 or AMD Radeon RX 6600 XT
7. DirectX Version: DirectX 12

Standard System Requirements:

1. **DirectX Version**: DirectX 12 Ultimate
2. **Processor:** Intel Core i9 (13th Gen) or AMD Ryzen 9 (7000 Series)
3. **RAM**: 32GB DDR5
4. **Operating System:** Windows 11 (64-bit) or macOS (latest version with Metal compatibility)
5. **Graphics Card:** NVIDIA GeForce RTX 4080 or AMD Radeon RX 7900 XTX
6. **Storage:** 1TB NVMe SSD (for faster loading times)

High-End System Requirements (For Virtual Production & AAA Game Development):

1. **Processor:** AMD Threadripper PRO or Intel Xeon

2. **Storage:** 2TB NVMe SSD + additional SSDs for project files

3. **Operating System:** Windows 11 Pro (64-bit) or Linux (latest)

4. **RAM:** 64GB DDR5 or above

5. **Graphics Card:** NVIDIA RTX 6000 Ada Generation or AMD Radeon Pro W7900

6. **Additional Hardware:** Dual-monitor setup, VR headset for VR development, and hardware ray tracing support

Factors that Affect System Performance in Unreal Engine 2025

1. **Nanite and Lumen Performance Impact**: These new rendering features require high-performance GPUs for real-time rendering.

2. **Chaos Physics**: Simulating large-scale destruction and physics-based interactions can be computationally intensive.

3. **Ray Tracing & Path Tracing**: Realistic lighting and reflections necessitate high-end GPUs with specialized RT cores.

4. **Memory Usage**: Additional RAM is necessary for large-scale projects to handle complicated environments and assets.

5. **Storage Speed**: SSDs (preferably NVMe) significantly reduce asset loading times and workflow efficiency.

Hardware Considerations for Unreal Engine (GPUs, CPUs, RAM, SSDs)

Unreal Engine 2025 will require high-end computing capabilities, especially for developers who are working on AAA games, virtual production, and large-scale simulations.

Graphics Processing Units (GPUs):

A high-performance GPU is necessary for rendering complex scenes, facilitating ray tracing, and ensuring smooth gameplay. Some important GPU requirements include:

1. **Minimum GPU**: NVIDIA RTX 3060 / AMD Radeon RX 6600 XT (suitable for indie games and basic rendering).

2. **Recommended GPU**: NVIDIA RTX 4080 / AMD Radeon RX 7900 XTX (for real-time ray tracing and complex game development).

3. **High-End GPU**: NVIDIA RTX 6000 Ada Generation / AMD Radeon Pro W7900 (for virtual production on a large scale and cinematic rendering).

4. **Key Features:** VRAM capacity (at least 12GB recommended), ray tracing support, and DLSS/FSR for performance optimization.

Central Processing Units (CPUs):

Unreal Engine (UE) leverages multi-threaded performance, so CPUs with high core counts are ideal for seamless asset processing and simulation. Some important CPU factors to have in mind are:

1. **Minimum CPU**: Intel i7-10700K / AMD Ryzen 7 3700X.

2. **Recommended CPU**: Intel i9-13900K / AMD Ryzen 9 7950X.

3. **High-End CPU**: AMD Threadripper PRO / Intel Xeon (for production pipelines and large-scale simulations).

Memory (RAM):

1. **Minimum:** 16GB DDR4 (for general development and small projects).

2. **Recommended:** 32GB DDR5 (for mid-sized projects and real-time rendering).

3. **High-End:** 64GB+ DDR5 (for virtual production, large worlds, and film-quality rendering).

Storage (SSDs & HDDs):

1. **Minimum Storage**: 500GB NVMe SSD (for basic UE files and projects).

2. **Recommended**: 1TB NVMe SSD (for increased asset streaming and real-time editing speeds).

3. **High-End:** 2TB+ NVMe SSD + multiple SSDs for project backup.

Guide to Set Up and Install the Unreal Engine

Prerequisites for Downloading Unreal Engine:

1. **Operating System**: Windows 10 64-bit or macOS 10.14 or later

2. **CPU**: Quad-core Intel or AMD processor, 2.5 GHz or above

3. **Memory:** 8 GB RAM (16 GB or more recommended)

4. **GPU:** DirectX 11 or DirectX 12 compliant graphics card

5. **Storage:** Solid-state drive (SSD) with at least 50 GB available space

These specifications ensure that your system can handle the heavy duty task of developing games. You can attempt to run Unreal Engine on a less spec'd machine, but you may notice some performance issues or longer compile times.

In addition to meeting the system specifications, you'll also need to download and install the Epic Games Launcher. The launcher serves as your entry point into the Unreal Engine universe, providing access to the engine itself, as well as to other Epic Games tools and services.

How to Download the Unreal Engine 5 from Epic Games Launcher

To download Unreal Engine 5, follow these steps:

1. Go to unreal engine.com and tap "Download".

2. In order to be able to install and run Unreal Editor, you need to download and install the **Epic Games** launcher. To download the launcher, you would see the **Download Launcher** button once you click the Download button on the Unreal Engine website.

3. After downloading and installing, launch the launcher and create or log in to your Epic Games account.

Now that you have installed the Epic Games Launcher, you can proceed to download Unreal Engine. Follow the following step-by-step process:

1. Open the **Epic Games launcher** and navigate to the **Unreal Engine** tab.

2. Select the version of Unreal Engine you wish to install and click on the "**Install**" button.

3. Choose the installation location on your PC. Select a directory with sufficient space to hold the engine and its supporting files.

4. Adjust the installation settings to your needs:

   o Turn on editor symbols for debugging to help diagnose the issue if the editor crashes.

   o Select the project templates and feature packs you want to install. They can form the foundation of your projects or contain specific functionality.

   o Assuming you intend to develop for platforms except for Windows or macOS, such as Linux, select the applicable additional platforms.

   o Click "**Install**" to start the download and installation.

   Note: Based on the stability of your internet connection and the features you've selected, this installation and download may take some time. Be patient and allow the Epic Games Launcher to do its job. When it's done, you'll have the full Unreal Engine set of tools and resources at your disposal.

Launching Unreal Engine for the First Time

With the Unreal Engine installed, you are now ready to launch the editor and begin working on your game. The first time the editor is launched, it will take a moment to configure any necessary objects that it needs. Once the editor does launch, it opens up with a window showing a list of template projects for various different industries, such as:

1. Games

2. Film

3. Architecture

4. Automotive

5. Product Design and Simulation

These template projects are excellent starting points, providing pre-set settings and assets for your chosen industry. Spend some time looking through these templates to gain a feel for what Unreal Engine is capable of. Once you're ready to begin your own project, you can create a new empty project or use one of the templates as a basis to work from.

Working With Unreal Editor and Key Toolsets

Below are the top 10 Unreal Engine tools that you absolutely need in your toolkit!

1. **Unreal Engine Editor**: The Unreal Engine Editor provides a robust interface for designing your games. From level design to asset management, this editor is your first stop in bringing your vision to life.

2. **Blueprint Visual Scripting**: Through this tool, you're able to create gameplay mechanics without writing a line of code. It's ideal for artists or designers who want to put functionality in place but don't want to be held back by coding.

3. **Materials Editor:** The Materials Editor helps to get the appearance of your game done. It allows you to construct intricate materials using a node-based system. This means that you can generate textures and surfaces that make your environments pop in no time.

4. **Niagara Particle System**: The Niagara Particle System lets you create stunning effects like fire, smoke, and explosions. It's also flexible, allowing you to create sophisticated particle systems for any scenario, adding visual storytelling punch to your gameplay.

5. **Sequencer**: This cinematic tool enables you to create cutscenes, control camera angles, and build dramatic narratives within your game. If you want to make your players feel like they are playing an interactive movie, mastering Sequencer is important.

6. **Landscape Tool**: It allows you to mold massive landscapes that can fit dense forests, mountainous terrains, and even massive deserts.

7. **Audio Mixer**: The audio mixer allows you to control sound effects, music, and even voiceovers, helping you craft a dense soundscape.

8. **AI Behavior Tree**: This tool enables you to specify complex AI logic without overcoding. You can specify conditions, actions, and create a hierarchy of behaviors that make your characters more realistic.

9. **Unreal Engine Marketplace**: The Unreal Engine Marketplace is a combination of assets, plugins, and tools created by other developers. If you want characters, animations and environment assets, this marketplace is a place that can save you hours of development time.

10. **Integration With GitHub**: Finally, but just as importantly, you should use GitHub Integration for version control. Whether you are working in a group or perhaps overseeing your projects by yourself? This tool maintains the accessibility and organization of your project. It's particularly useful when managing several project branches or reverting to previous iterations.

Chapter 4

Unreal Engine Architecture

The Modular Structure of Unreal Engine

Modules are the basic building block of Unreal Engine's (UE) software architecture. They encapsulate specific editor tools, runtime behavior, libraries, or other behavior in self-contained units of code.

Each project and plugin have a default main module, but you can also create other modules aside from these to organize your code.

Below is an explanation of module organization and how modules can improve your Unreal Engine projects

Advantages of Using Modules

Modules has the following benefits:

1. Modules enforce sound separation of code, providing a way to encapsulate functionality and hide internal details of code.

2. Modules are compiled separately as independent compilation units. What this implies is that only the modules that have been modified will need to be compiled, and build times on larger projects will be significantly faster.

3. You can regulate when specific modules are loaded and unloaded at runtime. This provides an avenue of optimization for the performance of your project through managing what systems are available and active.

4. You can include or exclude modules from your project based on some conditions, such as you are compiling for which platform.

How to Set Up a Module

Below is an overview of how to create and use a module from scratch. If you do so, then you will create a gameplay module separate from the main module that your project comes with by default.

1. Build a high-level **Source** folder directory for your module, and give this directory the same name as your module.

Note: It is possible to place modules anywhere within any subdirectory in your Source folder, at any level of nesting. This enables you to use subdirectories to organize your modules.

2. Design a **[ModuleName].Build.cs** file in the root directory of your module and use it to specify dependencies on other modules. This will enable the Unreal build system to locate your module.

3. Design a **Private and Public** subfolders in your module's root directory.

4. Design a **[ModuleName]Module.cpp** file in the Private subdirectory of your module. You can use this to give functions for initializing and terminating your module, and other standard functions that Unreal Engine uses to manage modules.

5. To regulate how and when your module is loaded, add configuration data for your module to your **.uproject** or **.uplugin** file. This consists of the name, type, supported platforms, and load phase of the module.

6. Insert your module as a dependency in your **Build.cs** file for any module that will use it. Note: This might be your project's main module's **Build.cs file**.

7. Create your solution files for your IDE whenever you modify your **[ModuleName].Build.cs** file or restructure source files across folders. You can do this with any of the following:

   o   Run the code GenerateProjectFiles.bat.

   o   Right-click on .uproject file, then choose Generate Project Files.

   o   In Unreal Editor, choose File > Refresh Visual Studio Project.

How to Understand the Module Structure

All modules should be put in a **Source** directory within a plugin or project. Note that the root module folder ought to bear the same name as the corresponding module.

There also has to be an **[ModuleName].Build.cs** file for each module in its top-level directory, and its **C++ code** in **Private and Public** folders.

The illustration below is an example of the structure of folders as recommended for a module:

- [ModuleName]
    - Private
        - [ModuleName]Module.cpp
        - All .cpp files and private headers
    - Public
        - All public headers
    - [ModuleName].Build.cs

How to Configure Dependencies in the Build.cs File

The "Unreal build" system creates projects according to **Target.cs** files in your projects and the **Build.cs** files in your modules, not according to the solution files for your **IDE**.

The IDE solution is generated automatically when editing code, but the Unreal Build Tool (UBT) will ignore it when compiling projects.

All modules require a [**ModuleName**].**Build.cs** file placed in the module's root directory for the Unreal build system to recognize them.

In your **[ModuleName],Build.cs** file, you need to declare class and define your module derived from the **ModuleRules** class. Below is an illustration of what a simple **Build.cs file** should like:

```
1    using UnrealBuildTool;
2
3    public class ModuleTest: ModuleRules
4
5    {
6
7    public ModuleTest(ReadOnlyTargetRules Target) : base(Target)
8
9    {
10
11   PrivateDependencyModuleNames.AddRange(new string[] {"Core"});
12
13   }
14
15   }
16
```

Note: While configuring your **Build.cs** files, you will be utilizing primarily the **PrivateDependencyModuleNames** and **PublicDependencyModuleNames** lists. You will put module names in these lists, which will make modules available to your module's code. For example, if you add the "**Slate**" and "**SlateUI**" module names to your private dependencies list, you can include **Slate UI** classes in your module.

What Are the Private and Public Dependencies?

You would utilize the **PublicDependencyModuleNames** list when you are making use of the classes of a module publicly, say in a **public.h** file. This will enable other dependent modules on your module to use your header files without any issue.

Further, you have to add a module name to the **PrivateDependencyModuleNames** list if they are being privately used, such as **in .cpp** files. Private dependencies should be used wherever possible since they can reduce your project's compile times.

Tip: You can make most dependencies private instead of public by inserting forward declarations inside your header files.

How to Use the Private and Public Folders

If your module is a normal **C++ module** (i.e., ModuleType is not External in your.uproject or.uplugin), its **C++ code** should be placed under the Private and Public subdirectories of your module's root.

However, these have no relation to the **Private, Public,** or **Protected** access specifiers in your **C++** source code. These are utilized to control the code of the module to be visible to other modules. In case you have these folders, all **.cpp** files have to be in the Private folder. But note, the **Header (.h)** files have to be in the Private and Public folders based on the rules below:

1. When you place a header file in the Private folder, its data will not be accessible to any of the modules except its owning module. Classes, structs, and enums here will be accessible to other classes in the same module, but not to other modules.

2. If you place a header in the Public folder, Unreal's build system will expose what it contains to any other module that has a dependency on the current module. External modules' classes will be able to inherit classes that are within the Public folder, and you can define variables and references with classes, structs, and enums from the Public folder. The Private, Public, and Protected specifiers will work as normal for functions and variables.

3. If you are creating a module that will not be built as a dependency for others, you do not need to use the Private and Public folders. Any code outside of these folders will behave as if it were Private. A good example of this would be your game's main module, which will likely be at the end of the dependency chain.

4. If you want to, you can also organize your code more with subfolders for both Public and Private. With each new folder you create inside Public, place a corresponding folder with the same name inside Private. Similarly, with each new header file you include in Public, make sure the corresponding **.cpp** files are always inside the corresponding folder within Private.

5. If you create new classes through the New Class Wizard within Unreal Editor, it will automatically handle parallel construction within these folders.

How to Use the Module in C++

In order to make a module available to the rest of your **C++** project, you need to create a class that inherits from **IModuleInterface,** then plug that class into the **IMPLEMENT_MODULE** macro.

For the barest installation, you can place a .cpp file under the Private directory of your module, and call it **[ModuleName]Module.cpp** where **[ModuleName]** is the name of your module. Afterwards, keep calling the **IMPLEMENT_MODULE** macro after every other **#include** declaration, but use **FDefaultModuleImpl** as the class.

Below is a pictorial illustration:

```
1    #include "Modules/ModuleManager.h"
2
3    IMPLEMENT_MODULE(FDefaultModuleImpl, ModuleTest);
4
```

However, note:

1. From the above example, **FDefaultModuleImpl** is an empty class that extends **IModuleInterface**. Hence, for a more complex implementation, you can define your own class to extend in **this .cpp file.**

2. **IModuleInterface** has several functions that fire when your module is loaded and unloaded, similar to the Startup and Shutdown functions in the "**GameInstance****class**".

How to Use Modules in Your Projects

Whenever you make a new Unreal Engine project or plugin, it will automatically create a main module of its own, which you will find in the Source folder of your project. You can add external modules to your project by adding them to the **Build.cs** file of your project's main module.

For instance, if you want to use the **Gameplay Tasks** system in a project called **MyProject**, you need to open **MyProject.Build.cs**, then add the "**GameplayTasks**" module as a dependency.

Note that, in order to compile as fast as possible, Unreal Build Tool compiles only modules in the dependency graph of your project. This means that if a module is not in any **Build.cs** files used by your project, that module will be skipped compilation.

How to Control How the Module Loads

You have to note that **Your.uproject** and **.uplugin** files have a Modules list that determines what modules are loaded into your project and how they are loaded.

When you recreate your project files, entries for your modules will be automatically generated in this list if they aren't already, provided that you have them included in the dependency chain. Entries on this list will look like the following in the illustration below:

```
1    "Modules": [
2
3      {
4
5          "Name": "ModuleTest",
6
7          "Type": "Runtime",
8
9    "LoadingPhase": "Default",
10
11      },
12
13    {
14
15    "Name": "ModuleTestEditor",
16
17    "Type": "Editor",
18
19    }
20
21    ]
22
```

Note: Majority of game modules will simply specify their Name, and specify their Type as Runtime. But, if their **LoadingPhase** is not set it will be Default. There are all kinds of other module types, loading phases, and other parameters that dictate on which platforms a module will and won't load.

Also note that the most common types of modules are Runtime and Editor, for in-game classes and editor-only classes, respectively.

Blueprint vs. C++ Programming

When you start a new Unreal Engine project, one of the first choices you'll have to make will be whether to use Blueprint or C++ as your basis. This choice has the potential to radically influence how you build your game, so it's important that you know the pros and cons of each model.

Also, both C++ and Blueprint are acceptable, complementary means of creating a game using Unreal Engine, and it is Epic's recommendation that they be used in conjunction with one another to take advantage of each's strengths. If you do not have a completely ironclad reason to only write in Blueprint, start a C++ project and enjoy the both worlds.

Blueprints

Blueprint is a visual scripting language that allows game developers to put the logic of their game together by connecting graphically represented nodes.

It's sort of like a humongous flow chart, where the order of the execution of the code can be followed through the graph, and what is happening easily understood.

A simple Blueprint graph.

Note: Epic Games' strong focus on Blueprint in their fourth engine release lowers the threshold of entry and allows non-programs to dip their toe in creating functionality, and provides an enormous and complete set of fully integrated tools for power users.

Advantages of Blueprints:

1. A great learning resource to become accustomed to typical conventions utilized in the game development industry, and how being a programmer thinks.

2. Serves as a solidly paced primer on how Unreal Engine operates.

3. It's far quicker to bring a prototype to life and to have your game into a playable form.

Drawbacks of Blueprints:

1. Some of the more sophisticated engine capabilities are unavailable or restricted.

2. Since it is a more advanced language in general, Blueprint as a rule will be slower than C++.

3. Dozens of nodes within big graphs may become clunky and difficult to read.

C++

C++ is a universal text-based programming language found in software all over the world, from the operating system you're using right now to a whole host of popular game engines. It is fast and powerful, and the backbone of the Unreal Engine.

```
187    #pragma region VRBounds
188
189    void AVRPawn::OnLeaveVRBounds() {
190        if (GEngine)
191            GEngine->AddOnScreenDebugMessage(
192                -1, 5.f, FColor::Cyan, TEXT("[AVRPawn] Player has left VR bounds"));
193    }
194
195    void AVRPawn::OnReenterVRBounds() {
196        if (GEngine)
197            GEngine->AddOnScreenDebugMessage(
198                -1, 5.f, FColor::Cyan,
199                TEXT("[AVRPawn] Player has reentered VR bounds"));
200    }
201    #pragma endregion VRBounds
202
```

An example of some C++ code from Epic's virtual reality pawn.

Advantages of C++:

1. Every one of Unreal Engine's features is available at the start.

2. Anyone who has knowledge of C++ is able to dig into the source code of the engine.

3. Will usually be faster, especially on low-level operations.

Disadvantages of C++:

1. There is a greater threshold of entry.

2. There is going to be more work initially in production to have your game up and going.

3. There is less of a safety net, so it is easier to crash your game and/or the Editor.

Things to Note When Creating a Blueprint-Only Project

Pros:

1. Blueprint is easy to use, well-documented, and simple to understand for new game code writers. It is the first programming experience for many, and serves as a gateway to more complicated programming languages.

2. Blueprint will walk you through how Unreal Engine would prefer to have you code your game, firing off alerts whenever you do something that will likely cause your game to hang or otherwise fail. It's a great introduction to how the engine will understand your commands and overall best practices.

3. It is much easier to turn your ideas into playable prototypes using Blueprint. It takes less time to compile, and you can actually work completely inside the Editor, and it's been designed to be modular. This means you can drag in whole sections of gameplay logic and drop them into your graphs at once. Using Blueprint, you're up and running in minutes.

Cons:

1. On the other hand, Blueprint graphs are very visual, i.e., they tend to take up a lot more screen space to represent the same amount of code. What takes 4 lines of code in C++, in Blueprint might cover your screen with nodes and wires all connected together. Things can very easily get unruly and lead to what many call "Blueprint Spaghetti."

2. Within a Blueprint-only project, much of the more esoteric (but by no means all that esoteric) functionality of the engine will either be strictly curtailed, or will simply not exist. This was arguably done in order to keep the process streamlined and avoid having more recent developers overawed by their range of nodes, but sometimes the options that Epic will cut from inclusion by default come across as pretty arbitrary.

3. From the very first release of Unreal Engine, Blueprint has traditionally been astoundingly slower than C++ – especially when it comes to low level functionality like mathematics.

This is technically still true today, and by and large working with Blueprint instead of C++ will make your game a fraction slower. Though, enormous work has been done to improve, and depending on how your game works this is or isn't a problem. You may not notice a difference in the performance of your game at all.

Things to Note When Creating a Blueprint-Only Project

Pros:

1. When creating a new C++ project all the tools, features and options of the engine will be available at your disposal right from the start. If you know what you are looking for, you will be able to find it.

2. If you're using C++, then you will have the ability to code in the real Unreal Engine source code and modify anything you wish. Of course, this is only for experienced users who are very comfortable with the language.

3. C++ code is generally a lot faster than its Blueprint counterpart, particularly when performing mathematical functions. This does not necessarily seem like a lot on small games, but on even moderately-sized projects there are frequently many thousands of mathematical operations occurring every frame. It adds up quickly!

Cons:

1. It has never been easier to learn how to program, but that doesn't necessarily mean it's an easy skill to learn. For a beginner, coding in C++ is generally not as intuitive as Blueprint. If you're new to game development, programming, or even Unreal Engine specifically, there will be a more significant upfront cost in learning the basics.

2. C++ projects merely need more lead-in time to get going. The process is less streamlined than Blueprint, and as a result there are simply more hoops to jump through, even for veterans.

3. It's the opposite side of the coin to getting to use every feature of Unreal Engine untroubled right from the get-go. It's just so much easier to accidentally break things. Blueprint's compiler will steady your hand and warn you before you do something dangerous, but in C++ you're assumed to know somewhat more about what you're doing. Great power, great responsibility and all that.

Combining Blueprint & C++

Having reviewed these two options separately, let's have a look at how they can be used together, and how their combined strength can be used to overcome their individual weaknesses:

1. You can use both C++ and Blueprint and reap the benefits of the broader access and faster iteration/compile time that Blueprint offers during prototyping, but when you're satisfied

you've proven your concept and you're ready to polish you can then move pieces of your logic into C++ as necessary.

2. With a little bit of C++ familiarity, you can 'expose' functionality previously inaccessible to Blueprint. By defining your own nodes in C++ that can then be dropped into your graphs within the Editor, you can easily add functionality to your Blueprints in a matter of lines.

3. It lowers the entry barrier for you and your team to implement game logic. Although there will always be space for programmers to write in C++, with the architecture and more advanced gameplay systems completed, your level designers and artists can create higher level things with Blueprint, like laying down triggers and triggering events.

How to Convert Blueprint to C++

1. If you'd like to port your Blueprint to C++, you can start by creating a **C++ header** file for a Blueprint struct or class using **Blueprint Header View**.

2. The generated **.h** file contains all of your Blueprint's variable and function declarations, but you must manually port your function implementation into the corresponding **.cpp** file.

Learning the Unreal Engine API and Scripting Framework

Unreal Engine offers a variety of scripting and programming options for your game, with flexibility and potential for developers. Some of the options include the fundamental method of programming in C++, Blueprints Visual Scripting, and Python scripting.

C++ Programming:

The C++ programming in Unreal Engine is just like regular C++, utilizing classes, functions, and variables. Every class is a template for a completely new object or actor that can be further wrapped with the Unreal Engine Reflection System. C++ programming is utilized to establish simple game classes that can be further developed and built upon by designers using Blueprints.

Below is an illustration of a C++ class in Unreal Engine:

```cpp
#include "GameFramework/Actor.h"
#include "MyActor.generated.h"

UCLASS()
class MYGAME_API AMyActor : public AActor
{
GENERATED_BODY()

public:
AMyActor();

protected:
virtual void BeginPlay() override;

public:
virtual void Tick(float DeltaTime) override;
};
```

Note that:

1. This class adds a new actor that may be instantiated within the game world.

2. The **BeginPlay** and **Tick** options are overloaded to provide special behavior at game start and for every frame update.

Blueprints Visual Scripting

Blueprints Visual Scripting is a rich feature tool that allows developers to specify gameplay objects in a node-based interface in the Unreal Editor1. It is designed to be simple to use even for non-programmers, enabling them to specify complex behaviors and interactions without writing code. For example, in Blueprints, you can create a quick script to bring an actor to the front using the steps below:

1. Design a new Blueprint class with respect to the Actor.

2. Launch the **Blueprint Editor** and add a **Tick** event.

3. Attach the **Tick** event to an **AddActorLocalOffset** node.

4. Select the offset value which determines how the actor will move forward.

Python Scripting

The Python scripting is used to add editor utilities to Unreal Engine's pipeline for production, such as asset management scripts. Python is only ever meant to be used during editor tooling and never at runtime. In the illustration below, we have provided a basic Python script to rename all the selected assets in the Unreal Editor:

```python
import unreal

def rename_selected_assets(new_name):
    selected_assets = unreal.EditorUtilityLibrary.get_selected_assets()
    for index, asset in enumerate(selected_assets):
        asset_name = "{}_{}".format(new_name, index)
        unreal.EditorAssetLibrary.rename_asset(asset.get_path_name(), asset_name)

rename_selected_assets("NewAssetName")
```

How to Balance Blueprints and C++

Utilizing Blueprints and C++ simultaneously helps them leverage each other's capabilities. Blueprints can be set aside for fast iterations and prototyping, while for performance-oriented code and nitty-gritty details, they can depend upon C++.

Chapter 5

Graphics and Rendering

Advanced Rendering Techniques (Ray Tracing, Path Tracing, "etc.")

Generally, graphics and visual effects depend on rendering in great part. Advanced rendering methods raise reflections, lighting, and image quality. Unreal Engine provides several approaches to create realistic images.

Ray Tracing

To provide reasonable reflections, shadows, and global lighting, ray tracing mimics the behavior of light.

Functions of Ray Tracing:

1. Replaces realistic light behavior.

2. Creates precise refractions and reflections.

3. Gets ambient occlusion and soft shadows perfect.

4. Via precise light interactions, improves material realism.

5. Tracking light pathways generates real-life lighting situations.

When to Use and Apply Ray Tracing:

1. Improves game and movie realism.

2. Produces realistic mirror and water reflections.

3. Raises architectural visualization's shadow accuracy.

4. Applied in automobile design for reasonable vehicle renderings.

5. Important for visual effects photorealistic CGI.

Steps to Set Up Ray Tracing:

1. Create a new project by launching Unreal Engine.

2. Navigate to Edit > Project Settings.

3. Navigate to Rendering and turn on Ray Tracing.

4. To implement modifications, restart the engine.

5. **Note:** For improved quality, turn on Ray Traced Shadows, Reflections, and Global Illumination.

Path Tracing

Path tracing mimics more precisely light interactions, hence extending ray tracing.

What Are the Functions of Path Tracing?:

1. It models indirect illumination.

2. Creates realistically correct shadows.

3. Generates excellent ambient occlusion.

4. Calculations of light paths using Monte Carlo methods.

5. Offers objective high-accuracy rendering.

How to Use and Apply Path Tracing:

1. Can be applied in film visuals and offline rendering.

2. Creates high-fidelity architecture visualizations.

3. Advances scientific models of light behavior.

4. Perfect for film-quality rendering, especially where precision is absolutely vital.

5. Used in virtual production for pre-visualization.

How to Set Up Path Tracing:

1. Go to Project Settings and enable Ray Tracing.

2. Navigate to Viewport and choose Path Tracing Mode.

3. Change sample count for improved picture quality.

4. For accurate light sources use **HDRI lighting.**

5. **Note:** Enhance the bounce count to maximize light interactions.

Screen Space Reflection (SSR)

SSR generates real-time reflections utilizing screen-space data.

What Are the Functions of the SSR?:

1. Dynamically generates reflecting surfaces.

2. Boosts metal, glass, and water reflections.

3. Works without using further lighting calculations.

4. Utilizing depth buffer data enhances performance.

5. Simulates reflections without calling for Ray Tracing.

How to Apply and Use SSR:

1. Fit for game rendering in real time.

2. Improves architectural vision reflections.

3. Applied in performances-sensitive contexts.

4. Used for creating dynamic surroundings.

5. Provides game cinematics realism without significant GPU use.

Setting Up the SSR:

1. Launch the Post Process Volume.

2. Navigate to the **Screen Space Reflections** settings.

3. Modify the Change Quality and Intensity Slides.

4. Note: For realism, enable Roughness-based reflections.

5. **Note:** Test many materials to guarantee correct reflection accuracy.

Global Illumination (GI)

GI uses the way light bounces between surfaces to provide effects of natural illumination.

Functions of the GI:

1. It can be used to stimulate indirect light bouncing.

2. Enhances realism in both indoor and outdoor environments.

3. Manages both dynamic and stationary lighting.

4. Helps to lower the need for baked lighting.

5. Gets automatically adjusted for varying light environments.

The Uses and Applications of the GI:

1. Applied in high-end gaming graphics.

2. Used for realistic sceneries, both indoors and outside.

3. Improves virtual production's dynamic lighting quality.

4. Perfect for VR uses where illumination is very vital.

1. Helps to lower the necessity for several light sources.

Setting Up the GI:

1. Navigate to Project Settings and turn on Lumen Global Illumination.

2. Launch Post Process Volume.

3. Toggle the Global Illumination Method to Lumen.

4. Change **Lumen Scene Detail** for tweaking performance.

5. Thereafter, test for natural outcomes under different light sources.

Temporal Anti-aliasing (TAA)

TAA averages frames to soften sharp edges.

What Are the Uses of TAA?:

1. Lessens aliasing and flickering.

2. Improves motion picture clarity.

3. Perfect for high-resolution rendering.

4. Reduces ghosting in scenarios with quick motion.

5. Increases the stability of minute elements like cables and fences.

How to Use and Apply the TAA:

1. Improves real-time application visual quality.

2. Found in VR experiences and cinematic sequences.

3. Enhances high-detail environments' edges.

4. Lessens rendering's high sample count necessity.

5. Increases object and landscape fine detail visibility.

Guide to Set Up TAA:

1. Launch the Post Process Volume.

2. Navigate to the Anti-aliasing method.

3. Choose Temporal Anti- Aliasing (TAA).

4. Change the **TAA Sharpness** to balance clarity with quality.

5. Turn on **TAA Upsampling** for enhanced clarity.

Virtual Shadow Maps (VSM)

High-resolution shadow maps in VMS help to increase shadow accuracy.

Functions of VSM:

1. Improves the smoothness and shadow resolution.
2. Minishes shadow flickering in moving objects.
3. Manages large-scale scenarios effectively.
4. Remove relics from conventional shadow mapping.
5. It supports complicated geometry free of appreciable performance degradation.

How to Apply and Use the VSM:

1. Can be applied in open-world games in great numbers.
2. Improves film production's shadows.
3. Enhances virtual reality depth perception.
4. Offers renderings both inside and outside excellent shadows.
5. Perfect for high-performance uses which requires precise shadows.

Setting Up VSM:

1. Navigate to Rendering under Project Settings.
2. Enable Virtual Shadow Maps
3. Change the directional light settings.
4. Change **Shadow Resolution** for clarity.

Subsurface Scattering (SSS)

SSS models light moving over transparent materials like cloth and skin.

Functions of SSS:

1. It increases character rendering's realism.
2. Manages several light sources.
3. It gives leaves, wax, and other soft materials, reality.
4. Lessens strong lighting effects on other objects and skin.

How to Apply and Use the SSS:

1. Applied in animations of characters and creatures.

2. Improves cloth, wax, and foliage rendering.

3. Fundamental for scientific and medical visualizations.

4. Applied in realistic film depiction for human figures.

5. Perfect for lifelike skin paintings.

How to Set Up SSS:

1. Launch Materials Editor.

2. Activate Subsurface Profile in the Material settings.

3. Modify the Translucency and Scatter Radius settings.

4. For absolutely realistic effects, mix with Ray Tracing.

Nanite Virtualized Geometry- Optimization Techniques

Designed as a virtualized geometry framework, Nanite allows you to build experiences and games with enormous geometric detail; we are talking billions of polygons—stuff that would often strangle a high-end gaming PC, but Nanite runs flawless as butter.

Using a revolutionary Level of Detail (LOD) technology and transmitting just the pixels that is shown on the screen, Nanite perform its magic. It's like having a really effective assistant that just provides what you require, when you need it. Still, there are things we can do to improve and ensure our games operate even better even with this fantastic technology.

Why Improve Nanite Geometry?

You might be wondering, "Why do I have to maximize anything if Nanite is so amazing?" Although Nanite is fantastic, it isn't a magic bullet. Hence, here are some of the many of reasons to maximize your geometry:

1. Improved performance on less expensive hardware.

2. Less burden on other systems, including physics and illumination.

3. Quicker load times.

4. Better general performance in the game.

Understanding Your Poly Budget

Knowing your poly budget is really essential before you begin optimizing. While still keeping decent performance, this is the greatest number of polygons you might have on screen at any one moment. Generally speaking, with UE5 you should maintain your polycount between five and ten million triangles every frame. Remember, though, your target hardware and particular game requirements will affect this.

Note: The UE5 console's "**stat rhi**" and "**stat render**" commands let you verify your polycount. These will separate out your render thread time and draw calls, thereby enabling you to spot places where you could be running over your budget.

Optimizing and Maximizing Your Meshes Using Effective LODs

LODs remain your friend even with Nanite. Although Nanite has its own LOD system, you may also generate bespoke LODs for your models. The secret is to strike a sensible mix between performance and visual appeal. Following the guidelines below will help:

1. Your base mesh should begin with the highest LOD (**LOD0**).

2. Reducing the polycount will help to create lower LOD. For instance, at every level, aim for a 50–75% cut.

3. Automatic LOD generating in UE5 can be achieved with the " **Simplygon**" tool.

4. In-game tests your LODs to ensure they appear decent and function as expected.

How to Combine Meshes Wisely

Combining meshes can increase performance and aid to lower draw calls, however, it is not advisable for one to overreach. This is because many meshes can cause less effective culling and larger polycounts. Follow the tips below to accurately combine meshes:

1. Share the same material and combine closely spaced meshes.

2. Avoid merging meshes requiring various degrees of detail or LODs.

3. For simple mesh mixing in UE5, use the "Merge" tool.

Note: Recall that the aim is to preserve effective culling while thus lowering draw calls.

How to Use Instancing for Repeated Assets

Instancing might be a great performance saver if you have objects like buildings or trees that repeat frequently. Using instancing lets UE5 produce many copies of an object with one draw call. Follow the steps below:

1. Create your instance mesh in the UE5 content browser under "**Create Instanced Static Mesh**".

2. Either manually or with the '**Foliage**' tool, place your instanced meshes in the world.

3. Change the culling parameters to guarantee just visible instances are produced.

Note: You are advised to use it sparingly, because instancing can drastically cut your draw calls. Hence, mix and combine instanced and non-instanced assets to keep things fresh as overusing instancing could cause loss of originality in your surroundings.

Material Optimization and Maximization

Performance may also be much improved by optimizing your materials. It is important to simplify complex materials that have lots of instructions, this is because they could become a bottleneck. Follow the steps below:

1. Replace intricate arithmetic/math operation with basic ones.

2. Use fewer textures and samplers.

3. Control variances using material properties instead of producing many materials.

4. Reuse common material setups by utilizing material functions.

Note: Keep in mind that the objective is to produce aesthetically pleasing yet also highly functional materials. Hence, always keep an eye on performance, and don't hesitate to get creative with your material setups.

Consideration for Level Design

Just as perfecting your meshes and materials are important, optimizing your levels is just as important. A well-designed level can operate faultless even with huge polycounts. Here are some level design pointers to consider and factor in:

1. Hide objects that are not visible to the player via occlusion culling.

2. To enhance streaming, break apart your levels into smaller pieces.

3. Do not use too many dynamic objects on screen at once.

4. Control object LOD in various sections of your level with Level of Detail (LOD) volumes.

Note: Designing ideal levels is somewhat of a craft. It calls for a strong awareness of the technical as well as artistic elements of game production.

Testing and Profiling

Without a mention of profiling and testing, no optimization manual would be whole. While testing guarantees that your optimizations are really enhancing performance, profiling helps you to find performance bottlenecks in your game. Below are the steps you can follow:

1. First examine how your game performs with the UE5 profiler. Do this by navigating to **Window > Developer Tools > Profiler**.

2. Search for performance issues like excessive draw call counts, spikes in frame time, and other issues.

3. Test your game on a range of hardware to guarantee decent performance on several devices.

4. Iterate on your improvements depending on test findings and profiling data.

Have in mind: Although they take some time, profiling and testing are vitally vital for guaranteeing optimal performance.

Common Mistakes and Pitfalls to Prevent

One might easily fall into certain typical optimization traps, therefore, here are a few things to be on the lookout for:

1. **Over-optimizing too Early**: Although it's tempting to get caught up in perfecting every small detail, a lot of work may be wasted doing so. First concentrate on the large gains; thereafter, don't hesitate to trade-off.

2. **Not Profiling Enough**: Understanding where your performance bottlenecks are requires profile. Use the profiler to direct your improvements; avoid depending on conjecture.

3. **Ignoring Creative Intention**: Though performance is crucial, it is not the only and ultimate thing. Optimize not at the expense of your game's appearance and experience. Work closely with your creative staff to strike the proper mix.

Practical Approach on How to Use the Nanite Geometry

Now let's apply all this theory in practice with the case study below. Let us assume we are working on a scenario from a thick forest. We first have far too large a polycount, and performance suffers. Here is one way we may approach maximizing it:

1. **Map the Scene:**

    We must first profile the scenario to see where our performance bottlenecks are. Do this by accessing the UE5 profiler and examine what is happening. In this scenario, we will assume that we have observed that our frame time is rising every time we gaze at specific portions of the forest and our draw calls are really high.

2. **Maximize the Trees:**

    Right now, our polycount is most attributed to our trees. First let us create some LODs for them. Based on our highest LOD, the Simplygon tool may create automatically lesser LODs. For our lowest LOD, we will also allow impostor generation to boost performance even further.

    Afterwards, the next thing to consider is instancing. We may utilize instancing to cut our draw calls as our forest features many often occurring trees. We will design an instanced form of our tree mesh and use the Foliage tool to project it into the scene.

3. **Improve the Terrain:**

   Additionally adding to our high polycount is our landscape. First let's start by lowering the tessellation on regions the player cannot clearly see. For more far-off terrain, we can also conserve polygons by using a lower-resolution heightmap.

   We can further lower our polycount with landscape LODs as well.

   Note: Let us use UE5's automated LOD generating for terrain, since it supports it.

4. **Maximize the Supplies:**

   Let us reduce our somewhat complicated tree and ground components. We can do this by cutting back on the textures and samplers we used in our content. Instead of producing several materials, we may also use the material options to regulate differences in our trees.

5. **Test and Iterate**:

   Let us lastly evaluate our optimizations and observe how they have raised performance. The "stat unit" command allows us to compare our frame times before and after our tweaks. Should our performance goals still fall short, we can go back and make further tweaks.

Lumen Global Illumination – Application Techniques

Lumen is entirely focused on dynamic global lighting and reflections. It replicates realistic lighting and reflections that change in real-time by combining ray tracing, screen-space data, and sophisticated algorithms. Below is an explanation of how Lumen Global Illumination works:

1. **Ray Tracing:** Lumen uses ray tracing to compile scene details including object placements and materials.

2. **Screen-Space Data:** To assist in the computation of global lighting and reflections, it uses screen-space data (which includes depth and normal).

3. **Algorithm:** Lumen uses unique algorithms to handle acquired data and produce the output.

Note: Though Lumen does uses the ray tracing technique, it is not a pure ray tracing. However, it uses a hybrid method combining many techniques. Also, lumen can run in real-time, even on hardware not typically supporting ray tracing.

How to Enable Lumen for Your UE5 Project

You first must activate Lumen in your UE5 project by following the steps below:

1. Launch your project in Unreal Editor.

2. Navigate to Edit > Project Settings.

3. Under the **Engine option**, locate and click **Rendering.**

4. Navigate to the Dynamic Global Illumination section.

5. Toggle the Dynamic Global Illumination Method to Lumen.

6. Note: You can also enable Reflections by choosing Lumen as the Reflection Method while you are here.

Having completed the steps above, lumen would be immediately activated in your project.

Lumen Settings Breakdown

It is important to dissect some of the fundamental Lumen settings you will find in your project settings and on your lights. This is because Lumen's performance and visual quality can be greatly affected by these settings, thus one should know what they mean.

Project Settings:

1. **Dynamic Global Illumination Method:** Lumen may be enabled using dynamic global illumination method. From here you can also switch to various GI techniques as distance field or Ray tracing.

2. **Lumen Scene Version**: This guides Lumen's general performance and quality. Usually a decent balance, the default number can be adjusted to fit the demands of your project.

3. **Lumen Resolution Scale**: Lumen's internal calculation resolution is scaled using a Lumen Resolution Scale. However, lower values can increase performance but may impair graphic quality.

Light Settings:

1. **Cast Shadows:** Determines whether this light contributes to Lumen's global illumination calculations.

2. **Indirect illumination Intensity**: Scales the intensity of the indirect illumination supplied by this lamp.

3. **Distance Field Shadow Distance:** Controls the distance at which this light utilizes distance field shadows instead of Lumen for GI.

How to Work With Lumen in Your Scenes

Here we will go over some basic procedures and ideas for maximizing Lumen.

Changing Lights and Objects:

Lumen's reaction to variations in your setting is among the coolest aspects about it. You can also move a light or mesh about, and see the illumination change in real time! This is great for iterating on your ideas since it allows you quick comments on how your modifications influence the lighting of the environment. Remember that Lumen's real-time updates might drain your system, particularly in intricate situations. Should you be having performance problems, you may momentarily disable Lumen while working on another aspect of your scene.

Emissive Materials:

Another approach to include illumination into your scene are emissive materials. They're fantastic for producing neon signs, illuminating items, or even mimicking light streaming through a window. To generate an emissive material:

1. Use the **Material Editor** to create a new material.

2. Insert an **Emissive Color** node to the Emissive Color input on the main material node.

3. Select the intended color and intensity for your emissive material.

4. Use the material on a mesh in your scene.

How to Maximize Lumen Performance

Although, Lumen can be taxing on your system, however, here are some ideas for maximizing Lumen performance to ensure your project runs without problems and smoothly:

1. **Limit the Quantity of Dynamic Lights**: Although Lumen can manage several, too many can affect performance. Where at all feasible, try to use stationary or fixed lighting.

2. **Use the Lumen Resolution Scale**: Lowering the Lumen Resolution Scale in your project settings will assist to enhance performance, but at the expense of some visual quality.

3. **Turn Off Lumen on Less Important Lights**: Not every light in your scene has to support Lumen. Disabling the Cast Shadows option will help performance for less significant lighting.

Note: It is ultimately all about balance. Therefore, to achieve the greatest outcomes for your particular project, you will have to blend settings and procedures in just the correct numbers.

Lumen Reflection:

Although different but connected to Lumen GI, Lumen Reflections offer high-quality reflections that dynamically adapt with your scene. Below, we will go over how to use Lumen Reflections in your projects and activate them:

How to Enable Lumen Reflections:

Navigate to **Rendering** in your project settings, and then activate **Lumen Reflections** by setting the reflection method to Lumen.

How to Work With Reflection Captures:

You will need to place Reflection Capture actors if you wish to use Lumen Reflections in your scenario. These players guide Lumen on computation and presentation of reflections. Follow the steps below to arrange a Reflection Capture:

1. Navigate to the **Place** menu, choose **Reflection Capture**.

2. Pull the actor into the scene where you want Lumen to be calculating reflections.

3. To influence the region which **Reflection Capture** covers, modify the Influence Radius.

Note: Multiple reflection captures can help you to cover big or complicated portions in your picture. Just monitor your performance; too many captures might begin to affect your frame rate.

Reflection Capture Settings:

It is important for you to know few settings on the Reflection Capture actor:

1. **Influence Radius:** Controls the region the reflection capture covers by means of influence radius.

2. **Resolution Scale:** Changes the reflections' resolution. Reduced visual quality may result in lower values even if they could enhance performance.

3. **Priority**: Finds the value of this **Reflection Capture** compared to other ones. However, the first to be computed will be higher priority captures.

Lumen and Niagara VFX

Lumen and Niagara VFX are a wonderful combination. Here we will discuss how to utilize Lumen to produce amazing, dynamic effects and illuminate your Niagara VFX.

Enabling Lumen on Niagara Emitters:

Check the **Cast Shadows** option in the emitter's properties to help you to enable **Lumen** on a Niagara emitter. This indicates Lumen to integrate the emitter into its estimates of global illumination. Your Niagara VFX should now be adding to the lighting of the scene when this enabled.

Creating Light- Emitting VFX

Creating light-emitting visual effects with Lumen and Niagara is one of the coolest activities you can do. You can also design a magical spell effect which can light up the environment. Follow the steps below to do this:

1. Create your **Niagara emitter** and create your **VFX** as desired.

2. Turn on emitter cast shadows.

3. Change the indirect lighting intensity to regulate the **VFX** scene contribution level of light.

Virtual Production and Lumen

Lumen has some fascinating features for virtual production workflows. For instance, for live compositing, green screen work, and so forth, its capacity to offer real-time, high-quality global illumination and reflections makes it a powerful instrument.

Using Lumen Alongside nDisplay:

Unreal Engine's method for building multi-display, real-time visualizing configurations is **nDisplay**. Virtual production frequently uses it to build large, immersive screens encircling a live set. Lumen effortlessly connects with **nDisplay** to provide global lighting and reflections over your whole display configuration.

In order to use Lumen with **nDisplay** just activate it in your project settings like we did in the previous subsection. Lumen will automatically generate real-time GI and reflections using your **nDisplay setup.**

Lumen and In- Camera Visual Effects:

Lumen also revolutionizes in- camera VFX. Even in live action, its updates let you view reflections and final-quality lighting straight in the camera. This enables more informed decisions on site and helps to lower the demand for expensive post-production activities.

In order to have a clear picture of how much this feature is important, think of a situation where you are still on site and you are still able to view the precise lighting and reflections that will be in your final shot. This underscores the Lumen's virtual production power.

Lumens Limitations and Workarounds

Though Lumen is a great tool, it has several restrictions. We will go over some of Lumen's present constraints in this part along with possible solutions.

1. **Issues of Performance**: Lumen may be taxing on your machine as we have covered throughout this guide. Particularly on lower-end hardware, complex sceneries including many dynamic lights and objects might cause performance problems. To fix this:

   o Keep your performance under control by applying the above discussed optimization suggestions.

   o To distribute the workload, try combining Lumen with other GI techniques as distant field shadows or ray tracing.

2. **Material Limitations**: Some materials and shaders might not perform as Lumen expects. Materials using complicated refraction effects or unique shading models, for instance, may not be totally supported. Should problems arise with a certain material, follow the steps below:

    o   Experiment with a new shading technique or material simplification.

    o   If the problem particular material, think about applying another GI technique—ray tracing or distance field shadows.

3. **Platform Limitations**: Lumen is meant to be platform-agnostics, hence certain systems may have stronger support than others. Lumen's ray tracing characteristics, for instance, might not be completely supported on every hardware. To guarantee the best results follow the steps below:

    o   At the beginning of the development process, test your project on the intended platform.

    o   If required, be ready to change your Lumen settings or apply other GI techniques.

Photorealism vs Stylized Rendering Techniques

In Unreal Engine 5, photorealism is essentially about producing images that pass for reality. This calls for realistic shaders, premium fabrics, and cutting-edge lighting approaches. Unreal Engine 5 brings various fresh tools that simplify reaching photorealism than it has ever been possible.

The Power of Nanite

One of the most fascinating elements of Unreal Engine 5 is nanite. It lets you straight into the engine import high-resolution 3D models with billions of polygons straight without using LODs (Levels of Detail). This allows you to design rather intricate settings with low effect on performance.

To utilize Nanite, just import your Unreal Engine 5 high-resolution models. The engine will automatically manage the optimization so you may concentrate on creativity instead of technological restrictions.

Lumen: Real-Time Global Illumination

Unreal Engine 5 also boasts Lumen, another innovative feature. It guarantees realistic and dynamic appearance of your sceneries by means of real-time worldwide lighting and reflections. Lumen ideal for producing lifelike settings as it automatically adjusts to changes in illumination.

Navigate to the **Project Settings** to make sure Lumen is checked so that it would be enabled. Afterwards, you can change the settings to precisely control the illumination of your picture.

High-Quality Textures and Materials

Achieving photorealism depends critically on textures and materials. Unreal Engine 5 lets you produce realistic and intricate surfaces by supporting high-resolution textures and powerful material shaders.

Use high-resolution pictures and normal maps to faithfully depict the minute features of your surfaces while building textures. These textures may be created using Photoshop or Substance Painter. Unreal Engine 5 also enables physically-based rendering (PBR), therefore enabling the creation of lifelike materials.

Advanced Shaders for Realism

Realistic materials can be created only with shaders. Unreal Engine 5 provides a large spectrum of shaders from which you may adapt to fit your requirements. With the correct shaders, you can attain a great degree of realism from metallic surfaces to translucent glass.

In Unreal Engine 5, the Material Editor allows you to build sophisticated shaders with nodes and graphs, this strong instrument lets you generate intricate shaders. Reusable shader components can also be produced using the Material Functions.

Post Processing Effects

The authenticity of your scenes depends critically on post-processing enhancements. Unreal Engine 5 provides anti-aliasing, depth of field, bloom, and color grading among post-processing tools. These impacts might enable your work to have a cinematic appearance and feel.

To apply post-processing effects, visit the **Post Process Volume** and change the settings to fit your requirements. The Post Process Settings let you further control the results.

Dynamic Weather and Time of Day

Your sceneries' authenticity can be much improved with **dynamic weather and time of day.** Unreal Engine 5 lets you replicate various time of day and weather, therefore enhancing the immersion of your surroundings.

Navigate to **World Settings** and change the options for weather and time to apply dynamic weather and time of day. Additionally, you can adjust the lighting conditions depending on the time of day, using the **Environment Light** option.

Creating Realistic Water

One of the most difficult materials to realistically depict is water. Notwithstanding, Unreal Engine 5 offers advanced features for realistic water creation—including reflections, caustics, and dynamic waves.

Navigate to the **Water Material** settings and change the options for reflections, transparency, and wave dynamics to produce reasonable water. Also, the Water Plane can help you replicate water in your sceneries.

Adding Real-World Data

Including actual facts can help your scenarios to be much more realistic. Unreal Engine 5 enables importing 3D scans, topography data, and satellite images as well as other data kinds.

Use the **Unreal Engine's Data Import** features to include actual data. For precise landscape representation, use satellite images; alternatively, employ 3D scans to produce finely detailed representations of actual items.

Optimizing Performance

Although photorealism is important, flawless experience depends on efficiency optimization. Level of detail (LOD) systems, occlusion culling, and instancing are just a few of Unreal Engine 5's several options for maximizing speed.

Use the **LOD System** to generate several degrees of detail for your models so as to maximize performance. Occlusion Culling can also help to conceal items the camera cannot see. Multiple instances of the same object can also be effectively rendered with instance calling.

Chapter 6

Game Development Workflow

Creating and Managing Assets (Quixel Megascans, Blender integration)

Unreal Engine transformed the process of making games and real-time rendering by providing game developers with high-level software to create photorealistic worlds. Quixel Megascans and Blender are two components of this pipeline. Quixel Megascans contains an extensive library of high-resolution, photorealistic assets, and Blender is a versatile 3D modeling application used for modification, optimization, and additional detailing before adding assets into Unreal Engine.

The underlisted are seven asset types and how to create, manage, and integrate them easily in Unreal Engine using Quixel Megascans and Blender. The assets included are:

1. Rocks and Boulders

2. Foliage and Trees

3. Ground Materials (Textures & Surface Details)

4. Props (Small Items & Ornamentations)

5. Buildings and Architectural Assets

6. Water and Fluid Surfaces

7. Decals and Surface Imperfections

Rocks and Boulders: Adding Realism With Quixel Megascans

Sourcing & Importing from Quixel Megascans:

Quixel Megascans offers an extensive collection of high-resolution rock and boulder assets that come with PBR (Physically Based Rendering) textures. To bring them into Unreal Engine:

1. **Launch Quixel Bridge**: In Unreal Engine, go to the **Quixel Bridge** plugin.

2. **Choose Rock Assets**: Select the desired rocks or boulders from the Megascans library.

3. **Download & Import**: Download them at Nanite resolution for high-end visuals or LOD optimized for performance.

Optimizing in Blender:

1. **Retopology:** If using high-poly, use **Remesh** or **Decimate** modifier from Blender to lessen the poly amount.

2. **UV Unwrapping:** Maintain clean UVs to prevent texture stretching.

3. **Custom Sculpting**: Sculpt out the rock formation for unique differences.

Integrating in Unreal Engine:

1. Use **Nanite** for efficient high-poly mesh rendering.

2. Utilize **Megascans Material** or modify shader properties for damp, moss-covered, or dirty looks

3. Toggle collision for play interaction.

Foliage and Trees: Dynamic Natural Environments

Importing Quixel Megascans Foliage:

Megascans includes high-detail trees, grass, and foliage. These are designed to optimize Unreal's Foliage Tool, which supports mass placement of vegetation.

How to Customize in Blender:

Trees and foliage need to be optimized due to performance reasonss:

1. **Poly Reduction**: Use Blender's Decimate modifier to reduce poly count with minimal detail loss.

2. **Custom LODs**: Create Level of Detail (LOD) models for different distances.

3. **Wind Animation:** Add a simple rig or vertex animation to introduce slight swaying effects.

Using in Unreal Engine:

1. Utilize trees and foliage with the Foliage Tool in an optimal way.

2. Wind effects can be activated through the use of Unreal's SimpleGrassWind node in the material editor.

3. For auto-generation use procedural foliage volume, due to the terrain.

Ground Materials: Texture & Surface Details

Quixel Megascans Textures:

Megascans has various ground textures such as mud, sand, gravel, asphalt, and snow. These textures include:

1. Albedo (Base Color)
2. Normal Maps
3. Roughness & Displacement Maps

How to Enhance in Blender:

1. Apply displacement modifiers to bring real 3D detail onto flat surfaces.
2. Build an easy tiling texture using Blender's texture painting function.

Using in Unreal Engine:

1. Apply **Blended Materials** to combine textures in real-time.
2. Activate **Parallax Occlusion Mapping (POM)** to get depth view on flat surfaces.
3. Utilize **Runtime Virtual Texturing** to combine ground textures with assets in real-time.

Props: Small Objects & Decorations

Props are used to deliver environmental storytelling. They are barrels, crates, ruins, debris, and small things that populate a scene.

Creating & Importing from Blender:

1. **Model from Scratch**: Model each prop using the modeling tools of Blender.
2. **Adjust Megascans Assets**: Blend assets together to create new variations.
3. **Bake Normal Maps**: Transfer high-poly props to low-poly without compromising details.

How to Integrate in Unreal Engine:

1. Utilize **Master Materials** to create dynamic variations (e.g., mossy, rusty, or wet props).
2. Activate **Physics Interactions** for movable objects.
3. Utilize **Nanite** for static, high-detail props without performance loss.

Buildings and Architectural Assets

Using Megascans & Blender for Structures:

1. Megascans provides modular walls, doors, and ruins.

2. Blender can be used to create custom architecture particular to specific projects.

Optimizing for Unreal Engine:

1. Utilize trim sheets to enable high-quality details without excessive polycounts.
2. Utilize modular design for flexible level construction.
3. Apply proper collision setup to prevent player clipping.

How to Enhance in Unreal Engine:

1. Utilize smart materials for dirt accumulation.
2. Utilize virtual textures for high-poly surfaces.
3. Apply lighting for dynamic levels.

Water and Fluid Surfaces

Using Quixel Megascans for Water Surfaces:

Megascans offers materials for ocean waves, wet surfaces, and puddles.

Custom Water in Blender:

1. Build a low-poly water meshes for performance enhancement.
2. Utilize Blender's baked animations from fluid simulation.

Using in Unreal Engine:

1. Apply **UE's Water** Plugin for realistic water bodies.
2. Activate **Caustics & Refraction** for a natural look.
3. Use **Flow Maps** for flowing water effects.

Decals and Surface Imperfections

Why Decals Matter:

Decals add realistic wear, dirt, graffiti, and damage to surfaces, providing visual storytelling.

Creating Custom Decals:

1. Utilize Blender's texture painting to create unique grime, cracks, and stains.
2. Export as transparent PNGs or RGBA textures.

Using in Unreal Engine:

1. Utilize **Deferred Decal Materials** for efficient projection.

2. Activate **Normal Map Decals** for depth shading.

3. Blend with environment using **Roughness** and **Opacity** controls.

Level Design and World-Building Techniques

One of the selling points of Unreal Engine is that it has robust level design tools, which can be used simply by developers to design intricate and compelling game worlds. From landscape shaping to prop and lighting placement, Unreal Engine provides a comprehensive list of features that make the level design process efficient and easy to comprehend. This includes planning, asset creation, optimization, lighting, and player interaction to provide a polished and cohesive world.

Basic Principles of Level Design

Before you start placing assets in Unreal Engine, it's worth learning the fundamentals of level design. A good level naturally directs players, maintains their interest, and achieves a balance between aesthetics and gameplay.

Key Principles:

1. **Player Guidance & Navigation**: Use environmental guides like lighting, contrasting color, and leading lines to direct players.

2. **Pacing & Flow**: Maintain a rhythm between action, exploration, and safety zones.

3. **Verticality:** There should be more than one level and differences in elevation to introduce depth and strategic gameplay options.

4. **Storytelling through Environment:** World-building needs to be a narrative told through props, textures, and background objects.

Pre-production Planning:

Don't jump straight into Unreal Engine; rather, diagram out layouts or use top-down maps to develop a concrete structure. The majority of designers use paper prototyping or other tools like Photoshop or Miro for planning.

Blockout and Greyboxing Techniques

What is Greyboxing?

Greyboxing (or blockout) is a technique of creating with basic geometric primitives (cubes, cylinders, etc.) to set the layout and motion of a level before adding high-level assets. This is used to enable designers to focus on game mechanics first before getting derailed by appearances.

How to Blockout a Level in Unreal Engine:

1. **Apply BSP (Brush-Based Geometry):** In Unreal Engine, go to **Modes > Place > Geometry** and use BSP brushes to block out rough shapes for floors, walls, and platforms.

2. **Test Gameplay Early:** Also, at the blockout stage, you can include a player character and test movement. Level scale adjustment if necessary.

3. **Repeat Quickly:** Use boxy placeholders instead of importing final assets. Iterate again and again until movement and flow are satisfactory.

Benefits of Greyboxing:

1. Faster level iteration

2. Helps to recognize gameplay bottlenecks early on

3. Correct scale and navigation before loading in assets

Note: When you have finalized the greybox, you can then start replacing plain shapes with Quixel Megascans assets or with custom 3D models done in Blender.

Asset Placement & Environment Detailing

After level blocking, the next step is placing assets and environment detailing.

Asset Selection and Placement:

Create buildings and interior with modular assets. Unreal Engine supports the following:

1. Quixel Megascans for high-fidelity photorealistic assets

2. Custom Blender models for unique designs

3. Marketplace assets for quick prototyping

Principles of Effective Asset Placement:

1. **Silhouettes & Readability:** Ensure objects are legible against the background, allowing easy navigation for players.

2. **Focal Points:** Use landmarks to give directions to players. Example: A tall-building tower, statue, or shining portal.

3. **Break Repetition:** Avoid "copy-paste" repetition of the same assets; use minimal rotations, scale variations, and alternate textures.

How to Add Small Details for Realism:

1. **Decals:** Add dirt, cracks, and surface imperfections.

2. **Clutter:** Add small props like barrels, papers, and trash to make the world look "lived-in."

3. **Vegetation & Nature**: Use **Foliage** tool for trees, grass, and natural elements.

Lighting and Atmosphere

Lighting is crucial to building immersive worlds. Unreal Engine provides powerful lighting tools to create mood, depth, and visual storytelling.

Types of Lighting in Unreal Engine:

1. **Directional Light** – Simulates sunlight/moonlight.

2. **Point Lights** – Used for lamps, torches, or lit objects.

3. **Spotlights** – Concentrated beams of light for spot illumination.

4. **Sky Light** – Includes ambient sky lighting in the scene.

5. **Global Illumination (Lumen)** – Realistic dynamic lighting with bounced light.

Best Lighting Practices:

1. **Apply Soft Shadows**: Avoid unrealistic, sharp shadows by tweaking shadow softness controls.

2. **Boost Contrast:** Mix warm and cool light to enhance contrast and atmosphere.

3. Insert Fog & Post-Processing: Use Exponential Height Fog for atmospheric depth.

A clear example of the above when used in practice: A horror game may use low-intensity lights, flickering effects, and heavy fog to build suspense.

Performance Optimization

A beautifully designed level is useless if it runs at low FPS. Optimization ensures the level looks great without sacrificing performance.

Techniques for Optimization:

1. **Level of Detail (LOD)** – Reduce polygon count for distant objects.

2. **Occlusion Culling** – Render objects not visible to the player.

3. **Nanite (UE5)** – Support high-poly assets without dropping FPS.

4. **Virtual Textures** – Minimizes memory usage for big environments.

5. **Baking Lighting** – Employ static or immobile lighting wherever possible to cut down on real-time calculations.

Interactive Elements & Gameplay Flow

Scripting With Blueprints:

Unreal Engine's Blueprint system enables designers to implement gameplay mechanics without coding. For example:

1. Doors that open when the player approaches

2. Destructible objects

3. Sound effect or cutscene triggers

How to Ensure Good Gameplay Flow:

1. **Never Have Dead Ends**: Never make players lose their way; utilize lights, paths, or landmarks to steer them.

2. **Reward Players for Exploration:** Place collectibles, lore items, or power-ups in side areas.

3. **Balance Combat and Exploration**: Create areas diverse and engaging rather than repetitive.

Advanced Techniques for World-Building and Landscape Tools

These techniques speed up development for large worlds.

How to Use Unreal Engine's Procedural Tools:

1. **Landscape Tool**: Create mountains, rivers, and terrain from heightmaps.

2. **Procedural Foliage Spawner:** Automatically spawn forests and grass.

3. **Houdini Integration**: Procedurally generate roads, buildings, and caves.

When to Use Procedural vs. Manual World-Building:

1. **Procedural:** Large open-world games like RPGs and survival games.

2. **Manual:** Linear levels where art direction and detail control matter (e.g., story-based games).

Physics and Collision Mechanics

No matter whether you are dealing with destructible environments, ragdoll physics, vehicle simulations, or simple object collisions, Unreal Engine has different tools at your disposal to generate realistic and optimized effects.

Learning Unreal Engine's Physics System

Unreal Engine utilizes the PhysX physics engine (for UE4) and Chaos Physics Engine (for UE5) to simulate real-world physics. The engines provide support for interactions like gravity, collisions, forces, joints, and destruction.

Key Components of Unreal Engine Physics System:

1. **Rigid Body Physics** – Applies Newtonian physics to objects, with realistic motion and collision.

2. **Physics Materials** – Establishes friction, bounciness, and physical properties of objects.

3. **Constraints & Joints** – Enables movement constraints and realistic object interaction.

4. **Chaos Physics (UE5)** – Provides destruction, cloth simulation, and soft-body physics.

How to Enable Physics for an Object:

To enable physics for an object, follow the steps below:

1. Select the object in Unreal Engine Editor.

2. In the **Details** panel, enable **Simulate Physics** under **Physics** section.

3. Modify Mass, Damping, and Gravity settings to control movement.

Collision in Unreal Engine: Advanced & Intermediate Techniques

The Fundamentals of Collision:

Collisions control how objects interact with one another in Unreal Engine. Every object in the world has a collision shape, which defines its physical shape.

Collision Presets in Unreal Engine:

Unreal Engine has pre-set collision options, such as:

1. **No Collision** – The object is not interactive.

2. **Block All** – The object blocks everything.

3. **Overlap All** – The object reacts to overlap events but does not prevent movement.

4. **Custom Collision** – Responses for different types of objects can be specified manually.

Types of Shape Collision:

1. **Simple Collision Shapes** – Geometric shapes like box, sphere, or capsule.

2. **Complex Collision (Per-Poly Collision)** – Does collision based on the actual mesh (performance costly).

3. **Custom Collision Meshes** – Imported from Blender or any other 3D modeling software.

How to Create a Custom Collision in Unreal Engine:

To make a custom collision shape, follow the steps below:

1. Launch the Static Mesh Editor.
2. Navigate to **Collision > Add Simplified Collision** and choose a shape (Box, Capsule, Convex, etc.).
3. Modify the collision size to match the object's geometry.

Collision Responses and Filtering:

Collision Channels are utilized by Unreal Engine to control how objects collide. Some examples include:

1. Make players walk on a surface but pass bullets through.
2. Make triggers that can detect when an object enters space.

This is done through:

1. **Block** – Object does not move when it hits something.
2. **Overlap** – Object detects an interaction but does not block.
3. **Ignore** – Object passes through but does not detect anything.

Simulating Triggers With Overlap Events:

To detect when an object is within a trigger volume, follow the steps below:

1. Insert a Box Collision Component to your actor.
2. In Blueprints, utilize the **OnComponentBeginOverlap** event to execute code when a player enters the trigger.

Physics Constraints and Joints

Physics constraints allow you to create hinges, sliders, and other jointed mechanics for natural object-to-object interaction.

Types of Physics Constraints:

1. **Hinge (Revoute) Constraint** – Used on doors, spinning wheels, etc.
2. **Slider Constraint** – Allows for linear movement along an axis.
3. **Ball and Socket Constraint** – Mimics ball joints (handy for use in ragdoll physics).

How to Add a Physics Constraint:

1. Insert a Physics Constraint Component to your actor.

2. In the Details Panel, limit components (e.g., two objects grasped by each other).

3. Modify angular and linear limits to control movement.

Below is a practical example using a Swinging Door:

1. Use a **Physics Constraint** between a door and its frame.

2. Constrain the angular limits to restrict movement to 90°.

3. Activate the **Motor Strength** for auto-swinging.

Destructible Meshes and Chaos Physics

Unreal Engine's Chaos Destruction System (UE5) allows you to create objects that shatter when acted upon by forces and collisions dynamically.

How to Create Destructible Meshes:

1. Import a **Static Mesh** into Unreal Engine.

2. Convert it to a Destructible Mesh (UE4) or add Chaos Geometry Collection (UE5).

3. Modify **Fracture** settings (e.g., pieces, break threshold).

4. Use **Physics Constraints** to govern destruction behavior.

Advanced Destruction Settings:

1. **Impact Sensitivity** – Determines the amount of force required to shatter an object.

2. **Fracture Pattern** – Controls how the object breaks.

3. **Cluster Groups** – Keeps pieces together until a force sufficient enough to break them apart.

Ragdoll Physics and Character Collisions

Applying Ragdoll Physics in Unreal Engine:

1. Launch the Skeletal Mesh Editor.

2. Insert a Physics Asset (PHAT).

3. Modify **Bone Constraints** to limit movement.

4. Enable **Ragdoll Physics** upon a character's death or falling.

Combining Ragdoll Physics with Animations:

To combine animations and physics easily:

1. Utilize **Physical Animation Components** to mix physics and animation.
2. Allow **Pose Matching** to avoid unnatural gestures.

Vehicle and Rigid Body Physics

Unreal Engine comes with a strong Vehicle System that gives car physics just like in real life, including:

1. Suspension, Tire Friction, and Engine Torque
2. Drifting, Acceleration, and Braking Mechanics

Setting Up a Simple Vehicle:

1. Import a car model with Skeletal Mesh.
2. Utilize the **Wheeled Vehicle Component** to establish vehicle behavior.
3. Setup tire friction and suspension for realism.

How to Add Physics-Based Movements to Objects:

For simple physics-based objects like a rolling ball:

1. Insert a **Rigid Body Component** to an actor.
2. Utilize **Apply Force** or **Add Impulse** to dynamically push objects.

Optimization and Performance Requirements

Physics simulation can be demanding on performance, so optimization is necessary. Optimization best practices for unreal engine physics include:

1. **Limit Active Physics Objects** – Too many physics-enabled objects cause performance issues.
2. **Use Simplified Collision Meshes** – Prevent collisions by polygon.
3. **Add Sleep Thresholds** – Don't make objects simulate if idle.
4. **Use LODs on Physics Meshes** – Distance low-pass physics.
5. **Prevent Unnecessary Simulations** – Like disabling ragdoll physics when characters are far enough away.

Animation and Rigging With Control Rig

Unreal Engine has revolutionized rigging and animation pipelines with Control Rig, a node-based system that allows procedural animation, dynamic rigging, and real-time motion editing. Unlike traditional methods that rely on the use of third-party tools like Maya or Blender, Control Rig provides an in-built solution within Unreal Engine, making character animation easier and reducing dependence on pre-baked animations.

What is Control Rig?

Control Rig is Unreal Engine's integrated rigging and animation system, designed to offer procedural animation and runtime character rig control. Control Rig allows animators to establish complex character movement without requiring an external DCC (Digital Content Creation) tool.

Key Features of Control Rig:

1. Node-based workflow similar to Blueprint, simple to use for Unreal Engine programmers.

2. Runtime tuning supports procedural animation and real-time interaction.

3. Inverse Kinematics (IK) and Forward Kinematics (FK) blending for precise control.

4. Event-driven animation systems that respond in real-time to game play.

5. Sequencer integration, supporting cinematic animation workflows.

Note: Control Rig provides both the capability to create and edit animations, allowing developers to build fully procedural or hybrid animations that blend baked animation with real-time tweaks.

Setting Up Control Rig

Creating a Control Rig Asset:

To start working with Control Rig in Unreal Engine:

1. Launch Unreal Engine and import or create a **Skeletal Mesh**.

2. Go to Content Browser > Right-click > Animation > Control Rig.

3. Choose the **Target Skeleton** for the Control Rig.

4. Launch the recently created **Control Rig Editor**.

The Control Rig Graph:

The Control Rig framework operates on a graph-based workflow like Blueprints. The main components are:

1. **Hierarchy Panel**: Displays the skeletal structure and controls creation.

2. **Rig Graph**: The primary working space in which nodes are connected to specify rig behavior.

3. **Details Panel:** Shows properties for selected nodes or controls.

Note: The Rig Graph contains a node-based architecture where you can define IK solvers, FK chains, and procedural motion strategies.

How to Build a Basic Control Rig

Step 1: Adding Controls

In order to be able to move character bones around, we need Control Handles:

1. In the **Hierarchy panel**, right-click on a bone (e.g., hand_r).

2. Select **New Control** to create a control handle.

3. Rename and assign control type (e.g., Transform for global movement control).

4. Modify **Gizmo** settings for enhanced visibility.

Step 2: Forward Kinematics (FK) Implementation

FK is utilized for natural movements where bones are in a parent-child relationship.

1. Drop the **Control Handle** on the Rig Graph.

2. Use a **Set Transform** node to manipulate the bone rotation.

3. Connect it with the execution chain.

4. Change Control Values in the viewport to see FK in action.

Note: FK is great for animating arms, spines, and tails, where there is natural movement required.

Step 3: Using Inverse Kinematics (IK)

IK allows the end of a bone chain to be positioned, with the system automatically solving in-between joint positions.

1. Insert an **IK Control** to the end of a limb (e.g., foot_l).

2. Insert a Two Bone IK node in the Rig Graph.

3. Connect the Effector Transform to the IK Control.

4. Modify **Pole vector** to define knee/elbow bending direction.

Note: IK is suitable for legs, arms, and other jointed structures that need precise placement (e.g., character feet staying on the ground).

Advanced Control Rig Features

1. **Space Switching (Dynamic Parent Constraints)**: In animation, objects typically need to dynamically change reference points.

   o Utilize **Parent Constraint node** to create a control switch parent.

   o Perfect for hand-grabbing, when a hand control flips between world space and an object.

2. **Procedural Animation Using Control Rig**: Procedural driving of animation can be done with Control Rig and eliminate the necessity of baked animation.

   o Use math nodes for oscillation or random movement.

   o Control facial expressions dynamically by applying procedural values to control transforms.

   o Insert physics-based animation, such as secondary motion on hair or tails.

3. **Control Rig Using Sequencer**: Control Rig can be used with Sequencer, Unreal Engine's cinematic tool.

   o Time-animate control values in Sequencer.

   o Mix Control Rig animations with existing keyframe animations.

   o Tweak imported animations using **Control Rig**, performing non-destructive edits.

   Note: This is a godsend for cinematics and cutscenes, enabling precise adjustments to animations without having to revisit Maya or Blender.

4. **Using Control Rig at Runtime**: Control Rig is not just for offline animation—it can also be used at runtime.

   o **Character Pose Customization:** A character's pose can be dynamically adjusted by the player.

   o **Procedural Locomotion:** Foot placement can be dynamically adapted to terrain.

   o **Interactive Elements**: Objects can respond to player input in real-time.

Control Rig Tips and Tricks

1. **Ensure the Rig is Modular**: Utilize different control layers for FK, IK, and procedural animation to keep it organized.

2. **Optimize Performance**: Prevent unnecessary computation by turning off unused nodes.

3. **Use Naming Conventions**: Simple control names avoid confusion, i.e., IK_Hand_L or FK_Spine_01.

4. **Test in Sequencer and Gameplay**: Verify your rig operates within pre-rendered and real-time settings.

5. **Use Debugging Tools**: Employ breakpoints and variable watches in the Rig Graph to identify problems.

Chapter 7

Using AI and Machine Learning in Unreal Engine

AI-Driven NPC Behavior and Navigation (AI Perception System)

Let us first define exactly what we mean by NPC behaviors before we go right into the specifics. To put it simple, NPC behaviors, i.e., that is, the choices and actions non-player characters (NPCs) do within a game, are simple motions to sophisticated decision-making procedures responding to the player's activities and the game environment can all be part of these actions.

Creating intelligent NPC behaviors in UE5 calls for scripting, behavior trees, and artificial intelligence systems all taken together. The engine offers a strong set of instruments to let you effectively develop and apply these behaviors.

Introduction to Behavior Trees

Developing intelligent NPC behaviors in UE5 mostly depends on behavior trees. They let you specify a hierarchical work distribution for which an NPC is qualified. Every chore might be a straightforward movement to a place or a more involved series of movements.

Guidelines to Creating a Behavior Tree:

1. Launch your UE5 project and head for the **Content Browser.**

2. Choose Create > AI > Behavior Tree with a right-click.

3. Give your behavior tree a clear, descriptive name—like **BT_NPC_Patrol**.

Note: After building your behavior tree, you may begin adding nodes to specify the NPC's actions. You may have a Selector node, for instance, that choose between attacking and patrolling depending on particular criteria.

How to Create a Simple Patrol Behavior:

First let us begin with a basic behavior pattern. This is a fantastic approach to become acquainted with behavior trees and observe NPC interactions with the game environment. Below is a detailed manual for creating patrol behavior:

1. Launch your behavior tree (**BT_NPC_Patrol**).

2. The root node should be a Sequence node.

3. Insert a **Move To Task** node beneath a Sequence node.

4. Set the **Move To node's Blackboard Key** from a vector variable reflecting the patrol point.

5. To cause a delay before the NPC goes to the next patrol location, add a **Wait Task node** after the **Move To node**.

Having followed the steps above, your behavior tree should like the illustration in the picture below:

```
Sequence Move To (PatrolPoint) Wait (2 seconds)
```

Note: To have the NPC constantly monitor the region, add more patrol locations and build a loop. Although, the above is a simple example, it demonstrates how you may create NPC actions in UE5 using behavior trees.

How to Add Decision-Making With Blackboards:

You must add decision-making ability if you want your NPC to be more intelligent. Blackboards enter this scene here. Blackboards are data structures used to hold game world information like player whereabouts, NPC health, and other pertinent data. Use these guidelines below to design a blackboard:

1. Right-click and select Create > AI > Blackboard in the Content Browser.

2. Give your chalkboard a clear, unambiguous name, for example, **BB_NPC_Patrol.**

3. Insert the required keys, for instance, a vector for the patrol location and a boolean for if the player is detected, however, you need to open the blackboard first.

4. Your chalkboard will be useful in your behavior tree for decision-making after you have it set up. For instance, you might include a Selector node that, depending on player detection, choose between attacking and patrolling.

Scripting Custom Behaviors

Though blackboards and behavior trees are great, occasionally you want more control over your NPC actions. Scripting helps in this regard. For scripting, UE5 provides Blueprints and C++ so you may select the approach most suited for your workflow.

For instance, imagine wanting to design a custom behavior whereby the NPC looks for the player should they not have been observed for some time. One may write this behavior with Blueprints or C++. Below is a basic Blueprints example:

1. Create a fresh **Blueprint** class from **AIController.**

2. Launch the **Blueprint** and create a custom event to set off when the player hasn't been spotted for some time.

3. Utilize the **AI Perception** system in case such search for the player is necessary.

4. If the player is located, change the blackboard key to reflect that the player is detected.

Note: Although this is a high-level summary, it demonstrates how you may utilize scripting to produce unique behaviors outside of what behavior trees by themselves allow.

How to Integrate AI Perception

UE5's AI Perception component is a great tool for increasing the awareness of surroundings among your NPC. It lets NPC perceive and respond to inputs including sights, sounds, and even smells—if you're feeling inventive. Use these guidelines below to merge AI Perception:

1. Launch your **AIController** Blueprint.

2. Insert the **AI Perception** element into the Blueprint.

3. Adjust the perception parameters including the detection radius and sense kinds.

4. Based on NPC senses, update the blackboard keys using the perception events.

Note: The AI Perception system, for instance, may track the player's entering of NPC line of sight and modify the chalkboard key. This lets the NPC respond to the player's presence and go from patrolling to attacking.

Testing and Iterating:

Developing intelligent NPC behavior requires iterative work. You will have to examine your actions closely and change depending on how they show in the game. These ideas offer guidance on testing and iterating:

1. Test your behaviors in real-time with the Play In Editor (PIE) mode.

2. Track any problems or surprising actions as you see how the NPC respond to various events.

3. If it is necessary to raise the NPC's intellect, change the behavior trees, blackboards, and scripts.

4. Proceed until you find the outcomes satisfactory.

Optimizing Performance:

Keep an eye on performance as you add increasingly sophisticated actions to your NPC. Complex AI systems might be computationally costly; hence you will have to maximize your actions to guarantee seamless gameplay. These pointers help to maximize performance:

1. Optimize **Pathfinding** and lower the processing burden using artificial intelligence navigation.

2. Limit the total AI processing in a scenario by having less active NPC count.

3. Find and fix performance limits with AI Profiling tools.

4. Think about offloading some AI computation to background threads using AI Tasks.

Advanced Techniques:

Once you've perfected the fundamentals of building intelligent NPC actions, you can investigate more complex methods to propel your AI forward. These concepts should help you get going:

1. **Machine Learning:** Train your NPC using machine learning techniques to enable more sophisticated judgements.

2. **Procedural Behaviors:** Generate actions procedurally depending on the game's context and the player's movements.

3. **Emotional AI:** Inserting emotional states into your NPC will help them to be more approachable and human-like.

4. **Cooperative AI:** Design activities that let NPC cooperate and coordinate their movements.

Reinforcement Learning Applications

Generally, Reinforcement Learning is a form of machine learning whereby an agent learns to make decisions by means of interactions with an environment. The agent acts, gets either rewards or penalties, and modifies its behavior to maximize the total benefit. Like teaching a dog, you praise excellent behavior and over time the dog picks to do more of that.

Within the context of Unreal Engine, the environment is the game world and the agent is a character or thing found within that universe. Also, learning ideal behaviors—like negotiating a maze, battling foes, or even playing a complete game of soccer—is the agent's objective.

Why Would Unreal Engine Use Reinforcement Learning?

Why should you be bothered about RL in Unreal Engine? Well, there are a couple quite strong arguments:

1. RL lets you design artificial intelligence (AI) capable of learning from experience and situational adaptation.

2. It helps the creation of sophisticated actions that would be challenging to manually write.

3. Realistic NPC creation helps to improve the gameplay experience by allowing RL to create more lifelike and erratic non-player characters.

Organizing Your Unreal Engine Environment:

Make sure your Unreal Engine environment is set up correctly before we go into the specifics of using RL. Here's a brief checklist:

1. Install the most recent Unreal Engine variant available from the Epic Games launcher.

2. Launch a new project or open an existing one where RL is to be implemented.

3. Ensure that all the required plugins—including the AI Module and any other pertinent tools—are installed.

Selecting the Appropriate RL Algorithm:

Selecting the appropriate RL algorithm for your project will be among the first considerations you have to make. Popular algorithms abound with advantages and drawbacks of their own. These are some factors to give thought:

1. **Q-Learning:** For discrete action environments, Q-Learning is a powerful method. Also, for small-scale tasks and novices, it's fantastic.

2. **Deep Q-Network (DQN):** This is a kind of Q-Learning designed to manage more difficult settings by means of deep neural networks.

3. **Proximal Policy Optimization (PPO):** This is a more sophisticated method fit for continuous action environments and complicated behaviors.

How to Implement Reinforcement Learning in Unreal Engine:

Now let us get our hands onto some real-world application. Setting up a simple RL agent in Unreal Engine can be done step-by-step, as outlined below:

- **First Step**: Create and Define the Environment

  Clearly defining the surroundings where your agent will work comes first. This covers the agent's acts, the game environment, and the reward system. If you were designing a maze-solving agent, for instance, the environment would be the maze, the actions would be motions (left, right, forward, backward), and the rewards would be either achieving the objective or dodging hurdles.

- **Second step**: Create the Agent

  The next thing you have to do is to create the agent. Usually in Unreal Engine, this is a character or pawn able to interact with the surroundings. You can develop your own unique class or leverage the built-in character classes. Make sure your agent possesses the required elements to view the surroundings and act.

- **Third step**: Use the RL Algorithm

This is the interesting part. You can develop your own implementation or utilize a pre-built library like **Stable Baselines 3 or RLlib**. The illustration below is a basic Python DQN agent setup:

```python
import gym import numpy as np from stable_baselines3 import DQN from
stable_baselines3.common.env_checker import check_env # Define the
environment class CustomEnv(gym.Env): def __init__(self):
super(CustomEnv, self).__init__() self.action_space =
gym.spaces.Discrete(4) self.observation_space = gym.spaces.Box(low=0,
high=1, shape=(84, 84, 3), dtype=np.uint8) def step(self, action): #
Implement the step logic here return observation, reward, done, info def
reset(self): # Implement the reset logic here return observation # Check
the environment env = CustomEnv() check_env(env) # Create the DQN agent
model = DQN('CnnPolicy', env, verbose=1) # Train the agent
model.learn(total_timesteps=10000) # Save the model
model.save('dqn_custom_env')
```

Note: This is a simple example; you will have to alter it to suit your particular agent and environment. However, it ought to provide a good beginning point.

- **Fourth step**: Integrate Unreal Engine

The next thing to do is to interface your RL algorithm with Unreal Engine after it is configured. Usually, this entails creating a plugin or script to interact with the Unreal Engine environment from your Python code. Tools like **UnrealCV or AirSim** will help you to enable this connection.

Below is a pictorial illustration of your integration code's structuring should look like:

```
import unreal_engine as ue # Initialize the Unreal Engine environment
ue.init() # Load the game world ue.load_world('YourGameWorld') # Create
the agent agent = ue.create_agent('YourAgentClass') # Define the reward
function def reward_function(agent_state): # Implement the.reward logic
here return reward # Main training loop for episode in
range(num_episodes): observation = ue.reset_agent(agent) done = False
while not done: action = model.predict(observation)[0] observation,
reward, done, info = ue.step_agent(agent, action)
model.learn(observation, action, reward, done) # Clean up ue.close()
```

Note: This is a simplified model; you will have to modify it for your own project. It should, however, help you to close the distance between your RL technique and the Unreal Engine environment.

Debugging and Refining Your RL Agent

Using RL in Unreal Engine might be challenging; hence you will inevitably come across certain problems. These are some pointers on troubleshooting and improving your agent:

1. **Track Training Development**: Watch how your agent performs during training. Should it not be improving, your reward function or action area may be the cause of trouble.

2. **Tune Hyperparameters**: Experiment with many hyperparameters including exploration rate, discount factor, and learning rate. Little adjustments add up to a great impact.

3. **Use Visualization**: Visualize your agent's behavior and the reward terrain to help you to better grasp what is happening. Here, **TensorBoard** and other tools can be really beneficial.

4. **Simplify the Environment**: If your agent finds difficulty, attempt to simplify the surroundings or divide the work into smaller, more doable chores.

Real-World Applications and Project Ideas

Let's discuss some real-world applications and project ideas now that you have a basic understanding of how to use RL in Unreal Engine. These are few tips to help you started:

1. **Autonomous Vehicles:** Teach an agent to observe traffic laws and negotiate a virtual metropolis, avoiding hazards.

2. **Game AI:** Create intelligent non-player characters (NPCs) that can fit many gaming environments and provide gamers a demanding experience.

3. **Robotics Simulation:** Unreal Engine allows you to replicate robotic chores such object handling or navigation in challenging conditions.

4. **Virtual Assistants:** Create virtual assistants able to generate tailored recommendations or help by learning from user interactions.

Note: There are countless possibilities of what you can do; the greatest approach to learn is via experience. Choose a project that piques your attention then start it.

Procedural Content Generation Using AI

Basically, it's a means of dynamically producing material for your game utilizing algorithms. This may be anything from landscape to adventures to even whole universes. The main benefit here is that you may create a lot of material with little hand work. It's like running a small manufacturing facility in your game constantly producing fresh ideas.

For example, think of previous games like Minecraft or No Man's Sky. Procedural creation in these games produces practically limitless universes. Not only about quantity, though; procedural generation may also provide your game a great deal of diversity and repeatability. Your experience changes somewhat every time you play.

AI-Driven Procedural Generation: The Future

Given all this, therefore, where does artificial intelligence fit? Procedural creation driven by artificial intelligence then advances the idea. You're creating material utilizing machine learning models rather than merely following set algorithms. These models may learn from data and grow over time, therefore producing increasingly more varied and fascinating outcomes.

Assuming you are designing a game using procedurally produced dungeons. Using conventional procedural generation, you might have guidelines for how dungeons are arranged. But with artificial intelligence-driven procedural generation, the AI can create its own original designs while learning from hundreds of dungeon examples. It might even pick up trends and looks you hadn't considered.

The Power of Unreal Engine in AI Driven Procedural Generation

Unreal Engine's capabilities make it ideal for procedural generation; it has been progressively adding more AI tools to its toolbox.

Unreal Engine's adaptability is one of the benefits for AI-driven procedural generation. To build your AI models, you may employ a variety of programming languages and tools; subsequently, you can include them into the engine. Unreal Engine also boasts a vibrant community and extensive documentation, so if you find yourself stuck you are never far from assistance.

Setting Up Your Environment:

You can set up your development environment after you have gotten the fundamental knowledge of machine learning. You will require the following tools:

1. A PC with a reasonable GPU (AI things may be really taxing).

2. Installed Unreal Engine; install it from their website.

3. A Python environment setup (Most AI work is done in Python.)

4. Some libraries for machine learning, such as **TensorFlow or PyTorch.**

Creating Your AI Model:

It's time to build your first artificial intelligence model after your environment is set up. This is where things may get really complex as there is no one-size-fits-all solution. What you wish to produce will determine the type of model you develop.

For instance, when creating terrain, you may apply a Generative Adversarial Network (GAN). These kinds of neural networks are fantastic for producing lifelike, natural-looking images. Conversely, if you are creating something more ordered—such as a dungeon—you may apply a different strategy based on a reinforcement learning model.

Integrating Your Model With Unreal Engine:

Integrating your artificial intelligence model with Unreal Engine comes next. This can be somewhat difficult as you will have to work out how to translate your Python code from C++ into Unreal Engine's C++.

Running Python programs straight in the engine is made possible by leveraging Unreal Engine's Python API. This will load your AI model and create content right on demand.

One more technique is to use a plugin like **UnrealCV**. Though it is somewhat more complex, you have far more control. It enables your AI model and the engine to interact in real-time, hence bridging their gap.

Difficulties of AI-Driven Procedural Generation

Although procedural generation powered by artificial intelligence is really strong, it is not without difficulties; one of the biggest is control. Creating material on demand might make it difficult to forecast what you will obtain. Unintentional outcomes or odd malfunctions might result from this.

Performance presents even another difficulty. AI models may be quite demanding, hence creating material on demand could cause latency or slowdowns. This is particularly true if you're working on a game for consoles or lower-end PCs.

How then can one go beyond these obstacles? Though there isn't a silver bullet, you can apply several techniques as provided below:

1. **Balancing Control and Variety:**

   One way to handle the control problem is via a hybrid strategy. You can combine hand-crafted and procedural material rather than producing everything mechanically. This allows you to take use of the variability that procedural generating presents while nevertheless exerting more control over the end product.

   Using constraints is another tactic. You can provide your artificial intelligence model certain guidelines or restrictions. This can prevent undesired outcomes and assist to direct the generating process.

2. **Optimizing/ Maximizing Performance**:

   Regarding performance, there are few things you can do. One is content pre-generating. You may create a lot of material ahead of time and then load it as needed rather than creating everything on demand. This can help slowdowns in gaming be lessened.

   You can also maximize your artificial intelligence model. This might call for anything from changing the architectural of the model to using more effective algorithms. Though it's a bit of a dark art, it can really make an impact.

Metahuman Integration and Real-Time Character Generation

Integration of MetaHumans with Unreal Engine allows virtual production teams, game creators, filmmakers, and developers to create, modify, animate, and render lifelike characters in real-time.

An Overview of MetaHuman Creator:

Epic Games' cloud-based character creation tool MetaHuman Creator lets users create very accurate human characters. It offers:

1. Really accurate physique and face details.

2. Customizable sizes, skin tones, and hair styles.

3. Completely tuned skeleton structures for animation.

4. Unreal Engine real-time rendering support.

Salient Features of MetaHuman Creator:

1. MetaHumans uses 8K textures, sophisticated skin shaders, and strand-based hair systems for realism.

2. Users using procedural customizing can change clothes, body proportions, and face characteristics.

3. MetaHumans come with built-in face and body rigs for flawless animation pre-rigged for motion capture.

Accessing MetaHuman Creator:

1. Launch MetaHuman Creator.

2. Sign in with an Epic Games account.

3. Start the browser-based editor.

4. Personalize and download your MetaHuman for Unreal Engine.

Importing Metahumans into Unreal Engine

You will need to import a MetaHuman you made into Unreal Engine. Qupixel Bridge, a plugin handling MetaHuman downloads and asset management, helps to simplify this procedure. The procedures for importing a MetaHuman are as follows:

1. Activate the MetaHuman Plugin available in Unreal Engine:

   o Launch Unreal Engine (UE5).

   o Navigate to Edit > Plugins and activate MetaHuman Plugin.

   o Quit and launch the Unreal Engine again.

2. Download Your MetaHuman via Qupixel Bridge:

   o Launch the Quixel Bridge.

   o Go to MetaHumans > My MetaHumans.

   o Choose and download your character.

   o Tap "**Add to Project**" to include into your Unreal Engine scene.

3. Analyze the Imported MetaHuman Assets:

   o Metahumans will show under **Content > MetaHumans**.

   o Assets comprise body, face, hair, clothes, materials, and skeleton rigs.

4. Position the MetaHuman in the Level:

   o Bring the **MetaHuman Blueprint** into the scene.

   o Press Play to view it in real time.

Personalizing and Character Editing

MetaHumans are incredibly flexible even following import. Developers may:

1. Change Clothing, Hair, and Skin.

2. Modify textures and tones of skin.

3. Change density, style, and color of your hair.

4. Change materials or replace clothes assets.

How to Edit MetaHumans in Unreal Engine:

1. Change textures using material instances—that is, add tattoos or scars.

2. Change face morph targets depending on minor facial structural modifications.

3. Modify hair physics and shading using the **Groom Hair System**.

Customizing With Blender and Maya:

1. For finely sculpted export MetaHuman meshes, use **Blender** or **Maya.**

2. Insert personal accessories like weapons, piercings, or spectacles or change UV maps.

3. Reimport altered assets into Unreal Engine.

Rigging and Animation for Metahumans

Although, MetaHumans are ready for animation and have complete-body rig. Unreal Engine has Control Rigs meant to simplify character animation.

How to Use Unreal Engine's Control Rig:

1. Without the need for external software, Control Rigs enable real-time animation changes in Unreal Engine.

2. MetaHumans can be animated straight in Sequencer (Unreal's animation timeline tool).

IK (Inverse Kinematics) Setup:

1. MetaHumans modify animation using IK Retargeting.

2. Preserves authenticity while enabling mixing and matching of several animations.

Using Prefab Animations:

1. Combine MetaHumans with Mixamo or Unreal Marketplace Animations.

2. Retarget currently available **Motion Capture (MoCap)** data onto the **MetaHuman Skeleton**.

Facial Motion Capture and Animation

MetaHumans are supported by Live Link Face, ARKit, and MetaHuman Animator.

Live Link Face for Real-Time Facial Capture:

1. Real-time facial motion capturing uses iPhone Face ID sensors.

2. Notifies Unreal Engine live face data.

3. Creatively generates expressive animations using MetaHuman's sophisticated facial gear.

MetaHuman Animator (UE5.2+):

1. This is a new tool for extracting video-based high-quality face animations.

2. Creates frame-perfect digital animations from actual expressions.

Other Motion Capture Methods:

1. Xsens & Rokoko Suits for entire MoCap body.

2. DeepMotion and Faceware for incredibly accurate facial capture.

Manual Facial Animation in Sequencer:

1. Use **BlendShapes** for keyframe face animations.

2. Create predetermined facial emotions with **Pose Assets.**

Optimizing MetaHumans for Performance

MetaHumans are high-poly models, hence game performance optimization is important.

Techniques for Performance Optimization:

1. **LOD (Level of Detail) Scaling:** MetaHuman automatically sets LOD (Level of Detail) Scaling to lower detail at a distance.

2. **Nanite (UE5):** This lets highly polymeric humans render effectively.

3. **Reduce Texture Resolution:** Lower 8K textures to 4K or 2K for mobile and VR projects.

4. **Simplify Hair and Clothing:** Use polygonal hair for performance instead of strand-based hair; simplify hair and clothing.

Optimizing for VR and Mobile:

1. For MetaHumans in mobile games use **LOD 1 or LOD 2.**

2. Turn off skin materials' high-detail **subsurface scattering (SSS).**

3. Lower hair strand density for improved VR performance.

Chapter 8

Virtual Reality (VR) & Augmented Reality (AR)

Setting Up VR/AR Projects in UE

Virtual Reality (VR) and Augmented Reality (AR) have transformed interactive experiences in gaming, training, simulations, and visualization. Unreal Engine offers robust features for creating immersive VR/AR experiences with high-quality graphics, physics, and real-time interactions.

Differences Between VR vs. AR

1. Environment & User Perception:

   o VR completely replaces the real world with a fully digital environment, meaning the user is completely immersed in a virtual space.

   o AR enhances the real world by overlaying virtual objects onto physical environments, and the user can still interact with and see the real world.

2. Hardware Requirements:

   o VR requires specialized headsets like the Meta Quest, HTC Vive, Valve Index, or PlayStation VR that have built-in displays and motion tracking.

   o Augmented Reality can be operated on a tablet, smartphone, or specialized headsets like Microsoft HoloLens or Magic Leap that use cameras to perceive the real world.

3. Interaction & Controls:

   o In Virtual Reality, the user interacts with the virtual world using controllers, hand tracking, or eye tracking. VR experiences often require motion controllers or full-body tracking for interaction.

   o In AR, the user is interacting with virtual objects through touchscreen gestures, voice, or gaze tracking since AR is generally on a mobile device or mixed reality headset.

4. Movement & Tracking:

   o VR tracks the user's entire head and body movement (6DOF - Six Degrees of Freedom) to allow for movement within an entirely virtual environment.

- AR is primarily tracking the location of the device (or user's hands/head in some cases) relative to the real world, with camera-based tracking or LiDAR sensors used to anchor objects in the real world.

5. Level of Immersion:

- VR is a fully immersive experience that closes off the user from the real environment. It is ideal for gaming, simulation, and virtual training.

- AR is a semi-immersive experience that continues to make users aware of their surroundings as it enhances it with digital information. It is more suited for real-world applications like education, retail, industrial training, and medical visualization.

6. Uses & Applications

- VR is mainly utilized for gaming, simulation-based training, virtual meetings, and creative visualization. It is popular in industries like entertainment, healthcare, military training, and real estate.

- AR has many uses in retail, navigation, industrial design, medical training, and interaction in the real world. It enhances productivity by overlaying useful information onto real-world objects.

VR & AR Support in Unreal Engine

Unreal Engine allows in-built support for:

1. **VR Headsets** – Oculus, SteamVR (HTC Vive), PSVR, Windows Mixed Reality, Pico, Varjo
2. **AR Platforms** – ARKit (Apple), ARCore (Google), Microsoft HoloLens, Magic Leap
3. **OpenXR** – An industry standard for cross-platform VR/AR development

Note: Unreal Engine 5 (UE5) is recommended for VR/AR due to its Nanite, Lumen, and OpenXR features.

How to Set Up a VR Project

Step 1: Enable VR Plugins:

Before a VR project is created, ensure the correct plugins are enabled.

1. Launch Unreal Engine and go to **Edit > Plugins.**
2. Enable the following plugins:

- **OpenXR** (for cross-platform VR support)
- **Oculus VR** (for Meta Quest devices)

- SteamVR (for HTC Vive, Valve Index)
  - **Windows Mixed Reality** (for HoloLens & WMR headsets)
3. Restart Unreal Engine for the settings to be effected.

Step 2: Create a VR Project:

1. Open Unreal Engine.
2. Choose Games > Virtual Reality template.
3. Select **Blueprint** or **C++** (Blueprints are perfect for beginners).
4. Tap Create.

Step 3: Configuring VR Settings:

For VR to function correctly, configure the project settings:

1. Navigate to Edit > Project Settings.
2. Activate **Start in VR** under VR Settings.
3. Set **Default Pawn Class** to **VRPawn** (or create a custom VR player).
4. Under **Rendering**, enable **Forward Rendering** (VR performance is better).
5. Make sure **Instanced Stereo Rendering** is enabled for effective rendering.

Step 4: Add VR Camera & Motion Controllers:

1. In Blueprints, create a **VR Pawn** with:
   - **Camera Component** (head-tracking).
   - **Motion Controller** Components (left and right hands).
2. Set **VRPawn** as the default pawn in **GameMode.**

Step 5: Play & Test in VR:

1. Click VR Preview in the Unreal Engine Editor.
2. Make sure your VR headset is plugged in and tracked correctly.
3. Adjust scaling, interaction, and locomotion for best experience.

Setting Up an AR Project

Step 1: Enable AR Plugins
For AR development, Unreal Engine supports: ARKit (iOS), ARCore (Android), HoloLens (Mixed Reality) and Magic Leap.

1. Go to **Edit > Plugins**.
2. Enable **ARKit** (for iOS) or **ARCore** (for Android).
3. Restart Unreal Engine.

Step 2: Create an AR Project
1. Launch **Unreal Engine**.
2. Select **Handheld AR Template** (under AR templates).
3. Choose **Blueprint** or **C++** and click **Create**.

Step 3: Configure AR Session
1. Open **ARPawn Blueprint** and check the **ARSessionConfig** settings.
2. Configure tracking for **plane detection, image recognition,** and **object tracking**.
3. Ensure **lighting estimation is enabled** for realistic lighting.

Step 4: Test on a Mobile Device
1. **For iOS (ARKit):** Use an **iPhone/iPad** with Apple's **ARKit**.
2. **For Android (ARCore):** Use a device with **Google ARCore** support.
3. Package and deploy using **Unreal Remote 2** or directly through **USB debugging**.

Input & Interaction Systems for VR/AR

VR Interactions (Motion Controllers & Hand Tracking):
- **Grab & Drop Objects:** Use **Physics Handle Components** to pick up and move objects.
- **Teleportation Locomotion:** Implement **NavMesh-based teleportation** for smooth movement.
- **Smooth Locomotion:** Map joystick/thumbstick movement to player motion.
- **Hand Tracking:** Enable **OpenXR Hand Tracking** for gesture-based interactions.

AR Interactions (Touch & Real-World Mapping):

- **Touch to Place Objects:** Use **ARTraceResult** to detect surfaces.
- **Hand Gesture Tracking:** (Magic Leap & HoloLens) Detect hand gestures using **Hand Mesh Components**.
- **Occlusion & Passthrough:** Enable **Passthrough Materials** for mixed reality blending.

Optimizing Performance for VR/AR

VR Optimization Techniques:

1. **Use Forward Rendering** – Boosts performance with single-pass rendering.
2. **Enable Fixed Foveated Rendering (FFR)** – Optimizes rendering for Oculus Quest.
3. **Reduce Polycount & Texture Size** – Keep assets under **50k polys**.
4. **Disable Unnecessary Post-Processing Effects** – Motion blur, bloom, etc.
5. **Use LODs & Nanite** – Level of Detail (LOD) models improve frame rates.

AR Optimization Techniques:

1. **Use AR Light Estimation** – Matches AR objects to real-world lighting.
2. **Reduce Shadows & Reflections** – Saves processing power on mobile.
3. **Optimize Mesh Collisions** – Avoid complex collision meshes for mobile AR.

Advanced Features (Hand Tracking, Mixed Reality, Passthrough, etc.)

Hand Tracking (OpenXR, Oculus, HoloLens):

- Enable **OpenXR Hand Tracking** in project settings.
- Use **Hand Component** for finger tracking and gestures.
- Implement **pinch & grab interactions** for realistic object manipulation.

Mixed Reality & Passthrough (Quest Pro, HoloLens, Varjo XR):

- Enable **Camera Passthrough** for blending virtual and real-world elements.
- Use **Depth API** to interact with real-world surfaces dynamically.

Deploying VR/AR Applications

Building for Oculus & SteamVR:
1. **For Oculus Quest:** Package as **Android (ASTC)**.
2. **For PC VR (Vive, Index):** Package as **Windows 64-bit**.
3. Upload to **Meta App Lab** for Quest-based distribution.

Deploying AR Apps (iOS/Android):
- **iOS:** Enable **ARKit**, package as **iOS build**, and deploy via **TestFlight**.
- **Android:** Enable **ARCore**, package as **APK**, and install via **USB debugging**.

Advanced VR Locomotion Techniques

Locomotion in VR is one of the biggest challenges due to motion sickness and immersion breaking mechanics. We've already covered teleportation and smooth locomotion, but here are some additional movement methods to enhance player comfort and control:

Arm-Swinger Locomotion:
- Players move by swinging their arms, similar to natural walking.
- Reduces motion sickness as movement matches natural gestures.
- Implemented using motion controller velocity tracking.
- Example: "Gorilla Tag" uses this for VR climbing and movement.

Hybrid Locomotion:
- Combines teleportation with smooth movement for flexibility.
- Ideal for players who prefer one method over another.
- Can be toggled in settings to allow users to customize their experience.

Artificial Locomotion Enhancements:
- **Vignette Effects:** Reduce peripheral vision when moving to lower discomfort.
- **Snap Turning:** Instead of smooth camera rotation, rotates the player in fixed angles (15-30 degrees) to avoid nausea.
- **Head-Based Movement:** Move in the direction the player is looking (useful for seated VR experiences).

All of these **can be controlled via Blueprints** or C++ scripting to allow players to pick the movement method that suits them best.

Advanced AR Tracking Methods

AR doesn't just place objects on flat surfaces—it can interact with the real world dynamically through different tracking methods:

Image-Based Tracking:

- Uses pre-defined 2D images as anchors to place AR objects.
- Great for AR museum exhibits, posters, or packaging.
- Unreal Engine supports ARTrackedImages via ARKit and ARCore.

Object-Based Tracking:

- Recognizes 3D objects instead of 2D images.
- Example: Holding up a real-world toy to display AR animations on top of it.
- Requires pre-scanned 3D object data for tracking.

Persistent AR & Cloud Anchors:

- Saves AR object placements between sessions (AR Persistence).
- Allows multiple devices to share the same AR space (AR Cloud).
- Used in applications like AR multiplayer games or collaborative design.

OpenXR and Cross-Platform Deployment

What is OpenXR?

OpenXR is the cross-platform VR/AR standard that ensures your game runs on multiple headsets without major rework.

Why Use OpenXR?:

1. Eliminates the need for **separate SDKs** (Oculus SDK, SteamVR SDK, etc.).
2. Supports **all major VR platforms** (Meta, HTC Vive, Windows MR, PlayStation VR, Pico, etc.).
3. Allows **easier maintenance** with a single development pipeline.

How to Enable OpenXR in Unreal Engine?:

- Go to **Edit > Plugins** and enable **OpenXR Plugin**.

- Under **Project Settings > Platforms > OpenXR**, enable supported features.

- Test with different headsets and controllers to ensure compatibility.

Cross-Platform Deployment Challenges:

- **Controller Differences:** Some headsets use thumbsticks, while others rely on trackpads. Use input remapping in Unreal Engine.

- **Rendering Variations:** Quest 2 may need different optimizations than a PCVR headset.

- **Performance Scaling:** Mobile VR requires lower polygon counts and textures than high-end PC VR.

Using OpenXR ensures your VR project is future-proof and works across multiple platforms without needing major code rewrites.

Tips and Tricks for VR & AR

Here are some additional high-level optimizations to boost performance:

Foveated Rendering:

- Reduces resolution in the peripheral vision while keeping the center sharp.

- Meta Quest and PlayStation VR2 support Fixed Foveated Rendering (FFR).

- Some high-end headsets use Eye-Tracked Foveated Rendering for dynamic optimizations.

Asynchronous Spacewarp (ASW) for VR:

- Oculus ASW reprojects previous frames to maintain smooth movement even if FPS drops.

- Essential for low-end VR hardware or when running on older GPUs.

- Can be enabled in **Oculus Developer** settings for Quest 2.

GPU Profiling & Performance Testing:

- Use **Unreal's GPU Profiler (Stat GPU)** to analyze bottlenecks.

- Check for high draw calls, expensive shaders, or excessive post-processing.

- Reduce **Overdraw** by using simplified **UI elements** and **lightweight particle effects**.

AR-Specific Optimizations:

- Reduce **Real-Time Reflections & Shadows** on AR objects to improve mobile FPS.
- Use **Dynamic Occlusion** to prevent AR objects from looking "fake" when they intersect with real-world elements.
- Enable **Texture Compression** (ASTC for Android, PVRTC for iOS).

UI/UX in VR & AR

Many traditional **UI elements don't work well in VR or AR**. Here's how to **improve user experience**:

VR UI Design:

1. **Avoid Flat HUDs** – 2D UI floating in front of the player breaks immersion.
2. **Use Diegetic UI** – UI elements integrated within the 3D world (e.g., menus attached to wrist, holographic panels).
3. **Use Large, Readable Text** – Small text is unreadable due to lens distortion.

AR UI Design:

1. **Use World-Anchored UI** – Keep menus attached to real-world surfaces rather than floating.
2. **Allow Touch-Based Interaction** – Mobile AR users expect UI to behave like native mobile apps.
3. **Consider Lighting & Contrast** – AR UI must be visible in both bright and dark environments.

VR-Specific Optimizations for Oculus, HTC Vive, and Playstation VR

Virtual Reality (VR) development presents unique challenges, especially regarding performance, latency, and user comfort. Unlike traditional gaming, where frame drops may be tolerable, VR requires a minimum frame rate of 90 FPS (or even 120 FPS in some cases) to prevent motion sickness and provide a seamless experience. Unreal Engine provides powerful tools and settings to optimize VR applications for platforms like Oculus (Quest, Rift, and future models), HTC Vive, and PlayStation VR (PSVR1 & PSVR2).

Performance Targets & Requirements for VR Platforms

Before kicking off with optimizations, it's essential to understand the hardware limitations and performance targets for each major VR platform:

Platform	Recommended FPS	Resolution per Eye	Recommended Render Scale
Oculus Quest 2	72/90/120 FPS	1832x1920	1.0 - 1.2
Oculus Rift S	80 FPS	1280x1440	1.0 - 1.2
HTC Vive / Vive Pro	90 FPS	1080x1200 / 1440x1600	1.0 - 1.5
PlayStation VR (PSVR1)	90/120 FPS	960x1080	1.0
PlayStation VR2 (PSVR2)	90/120 FPS	2000x2040	1.0 - 1.5

Achieving these frame rates requires aggressive optimization of rendering, CPU load, and GPU performance.

General VR Optimization Strategies

Regardless of the platform, the following **core optimizations** are essential for smooth VR performance:

Reduce Draw Calls:

- Use **Instanced Static Meshes** instead of multiple individual meshes.
- Merge meshes using **Unreal's Hierarchical Level of Detail (HLOD)** system.
- Reduce the number of skeletal meshes and animated characters in view.

Optimize Lighting:

- **Use Baked Lighting**: Dynamic lights are expensive in VR. Use static or stationary lights **with** baked shadows where possible.
- **Disable Unnecessary Shadow Casting**: Only essential objects should cast dynamic shadows.

- Use **Forward Rendering** (instead of Deferred) to reduce lighting overhead.

Use Forward Rendering Instead of Deferred:
- Forward rendering is **faster and more efficient** for VR.
- Supports **MSAA anti-aliasing** (better for VR clarity).
- Enabled in **Project Settings > Rendering > Forward Shading**.

Optimize Post-Processing Effects:
- Avoid expensive effects like SSR (Screen Space Reflections), Motion Blur, and Depth of Field.
- Reduce the use of **Ambient Occlusion** and **Volumetric Fog**.
- Use **Foveated Rendering** on supported hardware (reduces quality in peripheral vision for performance).

Reduce Poly Count and Texture Resolution:
- Use **LOD (Level of Detail) models** aggressively.
- Keep character and environment poly count **below 100k triangles** per frame.
- Avoid 4K textures where unnecessary—2K or 1K is usually enough.

Optimize Physics and Collision:
- Use simple collision shapes instead of complex ones.
- Reduce physics calculations—use **Approximate Collision** rather than detailed convex hulls.
- Reduce unnecessary ragdoll and physics simulations.

Oculus-Specific Optimizations (Quest & Rift)

Oculus devices require additional optimizations due to standalone hardware limitations (Quest 2) and PC tethering performance needs (Rift S).

Oculus Quest Optimizations (Standalone VR):

Oculus Quest 2 is a mobile VR device, so performance constraints are stricter than PC VR.

Use Oculus Mobile Renderer:

- In **Project Settings > Rendering**, enable **Mobile HDR** only if necessary (it impacts performance).
- Use **Multiview Rendering** for stereo performance improvements.

Enable Fixed Foveated Rendering (FFR):

- Reduces resolution in peripheral vision, improving performance.
- Enable in **Project Settings > OculusVR > Fixed Foveated Rendering**.

Reduce CPU and GPU Load:

- Keep **Draw Calls under 1000** per frame.
- Use **GPU Profiler (stat GPU)** to identify bottlenecks.

Use Oculus' Performance Tools:

- Use **Oculus Developer Hub** to monitor **Frame Timings**.
- Run and logcat to check performance warnings.

Oculus Rift Optimizations (PC VR):

- Enable **Asynchronous Spacewarp (ASW)** to reduce perceived frame drops.
- Use **Dynamic Resolution Scaling** to maintain frame rate.
- Optimize for **80 FPS**, as Rift S refreshes at **80 Hz**.

HTC Vive/SteamVR Optimizations

HTC Vive devices rely on **SteamVR**, which has its own performance tools and rendering techniques.

Enable Motion Smoothing:

- SteamVR uses **Reprojection and Motion Smoothing** to fill in dropped frames.
- Enable via **SteamVR settings**.

Optimize for Lighthouse Tracking:

- Ensure low-latency movement tracking by avoiding CPU-heavy processes.
- Reduce latency by keeping CPU frame time under 11ms.

Use SteamVR Profiler (vrcompositor):

- Monitors frame timing and identifies CPU/GPU bottlenecks.

- Run **vrcompositor** and check for dropped frames.

PlayStation VR (PSVR1 & PSVR2) Optimizations

PlayStation VR has strict performance requirements, as developers cannot rely on variable hardware like PC VR.

PSVR1 Optimizations:

- 90/120 Hz target is mandatory; frame drops lead to reprojection and motion sickness.

- Optimize for low CPU overhead, as the PS4 CPU is weak.

- Reduce **Draw Calls** and **Complex Materials**.

- Use **Checkerboard Rendering** if necessary for performance.

PSVR2 Optimizations:

- Supports 120 Hz and eye-tracking-based foveated rendering.

- Use **Dynamic Resolution Scaling** for performance stability.

- Leverage **Haptic Feedback** and **Adaptive Triggers** for better immersion.

Platform-Specific Rendering & Input Considerations

Each VR platform has different input and rendering quirks that must be optimized separately.

Oculus Input Optimization:

- Use Oculus' OpenXR plugin for better cross-platform support.

- Optimize for Hand Tracking and Controller Inputs (Quest 2+).

HTC Vive Input Optimization:

Use **SteamVR Input System** instead of Unreal's default VR input mappings.

Ensure low-latency response for Vive Trackers.

PSVR Input Optimization:

- **PSVR1:** Optimize for Move Controllers and DualShock for tracking.

- **PSVR2**: Optimize for Sense Controllers with haptic feedback.

Debugging & Profiling VR Performance

Use Unreal's VR Debugging Tools:
- **stat GPU** – View GPU performance.
- **stat unit** – Monitor CPU, GPU, and frame time.
- **r.ScreenPercentage 100** – Adjust screen resolution for testing.

Use Platform-Specific Profiling Tools:
- **Oculus**: Oculus Developer Hub, adb logcat
- **SteamVR**: vrcompositor, SteamVR Frame Timing
- **PSVR**: PlayStation Profiler (only available to licensed developers)

Augmented Reality Development With Unreal Engine & ARKit/ARCore

Augmented Reality (AR) is transforming industries by blending digital content with the real world. Unreal Engine, combined with ARKit (for iOS) and ARCore (for Android), provides powerful tools to create immersive and interactive AR applications. Whether it's AR games, architectural visualization, or real-time object tracking, Unreal Engine makes it easier to develop high-quality AR experiences with its Blueprint system, real-time rendering, and physics simulation.

ARKit & ARCore

ARKit is Apple's AR framework for iPhones and iPads, leveraging the power of LiDAR, TrueDepth cameras, and motion sensors to create accurate AR experiences.

Key Features of ARKit:
- Plane Detection (horizontal/vertical surfaces)
- Face Tracking (with TrueDepth camera)
- LiDAR-powered Scene Reconstruction (on newer iPads & iPhones)
- Motion Capture (full-body tracking)
- Object & Image Recognition

On the other hand, ARCore is Google's AR framework for Android devices, using camera tracking and environment sensing to place digital objects in real-world space.

Key Features of ARCore:

- Motion Tracking (SLAM-based, no special sensors required)
- Light Estimation (matches virtual objects to real-world lighting)
- Plane Detection (detects flat surfaces like tables & floors)
- Augmented Images (recognizes and tracks images in the real world)

Both ARKit & ARCore use similar tracking techniques, allowing developers to create cross-platform AR applications in Unreal Engine.

Setting Up AR Development in Unreal Engine

To start developing AR applications in Unreal Engine, follow these steps:

Project Setup:

1. Open **Unreal Engine (UE 4.27+ or UE5)**.
2. Create a **Blank Blueprint Project**.
3. In **Project Settings**, enable:
    - **ARKit (for iOS)**
    - **ARCore (for Android)**
    - **Augmented Reality Plugin (UE Native AR support)**

Enabling AR Plugins:

Navigate to **Edit > Plugins**, and enable:

- **Apple ARKit** (for iOS development)
- **Google ARCore** (for Android development)
- **Augmented Reality** (Unreal's cross-platform AR framework).
- Restart Unreal Engine to apply changes.

Configure Mobile Settings:

In **Project Settings > Platforms**:

- **iOS:** Enable **Metal API** and **ARKit support**.

- **Android:** Enable **Vulkan/ES3.1** and **ARCore support**.

Building an AR Application in Unreal Engine
Creating an AR Pawn (AR Camera Setup):

To control the AR view, set up an **AR Pawn**:

1. Create a new Blueprint >**Pawn** >**ARPawn**.
2. Add a **Camera Component** (this acts as the AR camera).
3. Set the **Pawn** to **Auto-Possess Player 0** (so it starts with the AR camera active).

This allows the player to move and interact with AR objects through their device.

Implementing Plane Detection:
Plane detection is crucial for placing AR objects on real-world surfaces.

1. In **ARPawn Blueprint**, add an **ARPlane Actor**.
2. Use the "**AR Line Trace**" node in Blueprints to detect surfaces.
3. Enable **Debug Mode** to visualize detected surfaces in real-time.

When the player taps the screen, the system will identify a surface and place an AR object at that location.

Placing Objects in AR:
1. Create a Blueprint for an AR Object (e.g., a 3D model).
2. In the **ARPawn Blueprint**, create a **Spawn Actor** in the **Hit Location** function.
3. Set the actor to spawn when the user taps on a detected plane.
4. This creates a basic AR interaction, where users can place objects in their environment.

Advanced AR Features in Unreal Engine

Light Estimation (Matching Virtual Objects to Real-World Lighting):
To make AR objects appear more realistic, enable **Light Estimation**:

1. In Blueprints, use "**Get AR Light Estimate**".
2. Apply the **Light Intensity** and **Color** to AR objects dynamically.

Image Tracking (Augmented Images):

Image tracking allows AR applications to **recognize and track real-world images** (e.g., posters, product packaging).

1. In **Project Settings > Augmented Reality**, add **Reference Images** (JPG/PNG).

2. Create an **ARTrackedImage Actor**.

3. When Unreal detects an image, it can spawn a 3D model or trigger an animation.

Face Tracking (ARKit-Exclusive Feature):

For iPhones/iPads with Face ID, ARKit can track facial expressions:

1. Enable **Face Tracking** in ARKit settings.

2. Use an **ARFaceMesh Component** to apply animations to a virtual face.

3. Map expressions to a **3D avatar** in Unreal Engine.

This is useful for AR filters, facial animation, and social AR applications.

LiDAR-Based Scene Reconstruction (ARKit on iPad Pro & iPhone Pro Models):

Newer Apple devices with **LiDAR sensors** can create **detailed 3D maps of the environment**.

- Use ARKit Scene Reconstruction to generate real-time meshes of the surroundings.

- This enables physics-based interactions with real-world objects.

Mixed Reality Applications and Trends

Mixed Reality (MR) refers to experiences where virtual content is anchored and interacts with the real world, bridging the gap between AR and VR. Unlike AR, MR doesn't just overlay objects—it allows them to respond to real-world physics, occlusion, and lighting.

Below are what Mixed Reality applications rely on:

- Spatial Mapping & Environment Understanding (scanning real-world environments for interaction).

- Hand & Eye Tracking (for more natural interaction with virtual elements).

- Occlusion & Depth Sensing (to make digital objects behave realistically).

- Cloud-based MR (to persist objects across multiple users and devices).

Also, several hardware platforms support MR development in Unreal Engine:

1. **Microsoft HoloLens 2** – A standalone MR headset with advanced hand tracking, eye tracking, and spatial mapping. Used mainly for enterprise applications in healthcare, manufacturing, and remote collaboration.

2. **Meta Quest 3** – A VR/MR hybrid headset featuring high-quality passthrough AR, room mapping, and hand-tracking capabilities, making it ideal for gaming and productivity applications.

3. **Magic Leap 2** – An enterprise-focused MR headset offering spatial computing, real-time occlusion, and precision hand-tracking for industrial, medical, and creative applications.

4. **Apple Vision Pro** – A high-end MR headset with ultra-high-resolution displays, advanced eye-tracking, and seamless AR integration, designed for productivity, immersive experiences, and digital workspace enhancements.

5. **Meta Quest Pro** – A more powerful variant of the Quest series, designed for business and professional applications, featuring color passthrough AR, face tracking, and improved MR interaction.

6. **Varjo XR-4** – A high-fidelity MR headset used for professional simulation, aerospace, and medical applications, known for its ultra-realistic graphics and eye-tracking features.

7. **Lenovo ThinkReality A3** – A lightweight MR headset designed for enterprise use, enabling AR overlays and spatial computing in industrial and business settings.

8. **Snapdragon XR2-Based Headsets** – Various MR headsets from manufacturers like HTC, Pico, and others, powered by Qualcomm's XR2 chipset, offering passthrough AR and spatial computing for different use cases.

Setting Up an MR Project in Unreal Engine

To develop MR applications:

1. **Install the Required Plugins**:
   - Microsoft Mixed Reality Plugin (for HoloLens).
   - ARKit & ARCore Plugins (for MR on mobile devices).
   - OpenXR Plugin (for Meta Quest, Magic Leap, and Vision Pro).

2. **Enable Passthrough & Spatial Mapping:**
   - Passthrough enables real-world visibility inside VR headsets.
   - Spatial Mapping scans the user's environment for real-time interaction with virtual objects.

3. **Set Up MR Camera & Tracking:**
   - Use the **ARPawn** or **XRPlayerController** to handle camera tracking.

o Enable **Hand & Eye Tracking** for gesture-based controls.

Features of MR Development in Unreal Engine

1. **Passthrough AR & Environment Mapping:** Passthrough allows users to see the real world while interacting with virtual elements.

   o Meta Quest Pro & Quest 3 use color passthrough for blending digital and real-world visuals.

   o Unreal Engine supports Occlusion & Depth-based Rendering for realistic MR effects.

2. **Hand & Eye Tracking in MR:**

   o HoloLens 2 & Vision Pro provide native hand and eye tracking, enabling gesture-based interactions.

   o Unreal Engine's XR Interaction System allows developers to use pinch, grab, and drag gestures.

3. **Spatial Anchors & Persistent MR Experiences:**

   o Spatial Anchors allow users to place digital objects persistently in real-world locations.

   o Using Cloud Anchors (ARKit, ARCore, or Azure Spatial Anchors) allows multi-user MR experiences.

4. **Physics-Based MR Interactions:**

   o Unreal's Chaos Physics Engine enables realistic collisions between virtual and real-world objects.

   o Objects can respond to gravity, forces, and user interactions dynamically.

5. **Multi-Device & Cross-Platform MR Development:**

   o Unreal's OpenXR Support allows development across Quest, HoloLens, Magic Leap, and Vision Pro.

   o The MR Remote Framework enables developers to stream MR experiences from a PC to an MR headset.

Applications of Mixed Reality

1. **Mixed Reality in Gaming & Entertainment:**

   o **Real-World Object Interaction**: Games like Demeo XR (Quest 3) **use** Passthrough AR for tabletop gaming.

- o **MR Escape Rooms & Horror Experiences**: Users navigate real spaces enhanced with virtual effects.
- o **Interactive Storytelling**: Games blend CGI characters with the player's real-world environment.

2. **Mixed Reality in Architecture & Design:**
   - o Real-time 3D modeling in physical space (HoloLens 2 & Magic Leap 2).
   - o **Live Architectural Visualization**: Walk through **real-sized 3D buildings** before construction.
   - o **Collaboration Tools**: Multiple designers interact with the same MR model remotely.

3. **Mixed Reality in Healthcare & Medical Training:**
   - o **Surgical Simulations**: MR overlays medical data on a real patient's body.
   - o **HoloLens-based Remote Assistance**: Surgeons can guide procedures in real-time.
   - o **Anatomy Education**: Medical students interact with life-sized 3D anatomy models.

4. **Mixed Reality in Industrial Training & Remote Assistance:**
   - o **Hands-Free Instructions**: MR guides technicians **through** complex machinery repairs.
   - o **Augmented Workspaces**: Digital schematics overlay onto real-world equipment.
   - o **Remote Collaboration**: Engineers & workers interact with virtual prototypes in real-time.

5. **Mixed Reality in Retail & E-commerce:**
   - o **Virtual Product Showrooms**: Customers visualize furniture, clothing, or electronics in their home.
   - o **Try-before-you-buy Experiences**: MR allows users to preview car models, glasses, or shoes in real-world settings.
   - o **Interactive Shopping**: Stores create immersive brand experiences with MR product demos.

Chapter 9

Multiplayer & Online Game Development

How to utilize Unreal Engine's Networking Framework (Replication, Sessions, etc.)

Unreal Engine's network system allows game developers to develop multiplayer games using a solid client-server architecture. Below are the benefits of using Unreal Engine's in-built networking:

1. Manages Replication Automatically

2. Supports Dedicated and Listen Servers

3. Built-in Multiplayer Session Handling (Steam, EOS, etc.)

4. Enhanced Blueprint Integration for Multiplayer

Getting Started with Unreal Engine's Networking Model

Here are some fundamentals of Unreal Engine's network system

1. Unreal Engine Uses a Client-Server Model:

   o **Dedicated Server**: A server-side headless run on a server machine (appropriately designed for big-scale multiplayer games).

   o **Listen Server**: One player operates the server but also plays the game.

   o **Clients:** Players who log in to the server to receive game updates.

2. Important Networking Concepts:

   o **Replication:** Syncing server data to connected clients.

   o **Authority**: The server maintains control of important game logic (clients cannot make important changes).

   o **RPCs (Remote Procedure Calls):** Used to call function calls from the server to clients.

Creating a Multiplayer Project

Firstly, you need to configure Unreal Engine properly before implementing the networking features.

How to Enable Networking:

1. Start Unreal Engine.

2. Navigate to Edit > Project Settings > Maps & Modes.

3. In the **GameMode** option, set **Default GameMode** to **GameModeBase** or a custom multiplayer GameMode.

4. Navigate down to **Network Settings**:

   o Activate **Seamless Travel** (Allows smooth transition between levels).

   o Utilize Dedicated Server if running a standalone server.

How to Create a Multiplayer Map:

1. Navigate to **File > New Level** and create a basic game map.

2. Insert a **Player Start** object (needed for spawning players).

3. Save it as **MP_Map** in your project.

Setting Up Networked Player Character:

1. Enable a new Blueprint Class from Character.

2. Check Replicates in the Class Defaults window.

3. Insert a Static Mesh Component and check Replicate Movement.

Using Replication to Sync Data Across Clients

Replication is utilized to ensure that critical data is synchronized across all connected players.

Unreal Engine enables replication on:

1. Variables (Properties)

2. Functions (RPCs)

3. Actors and Components

How to Replicate Variables (For Example, Syncing Player Health):

1. Launch your PlayerCharacter Blueprint.

2. Add a Health variable (Float, default 100).

3. In the **Details** panel, turn on **Replicated.**

4. Insert an event:

- o On **Take Damage**, this subtracts from Health.
- o Make sure the logic runs on the Server (Authority Check).

Below are some examples of Blueprint (Health Syncing):

1. The server is responsible for controlling Health and updates it.
2. Clients automatically get the updated Health.

Using RPCs (Remote Procedure Calls) for Multiplayer

Replication synchronizes, but sometimes you need to call functions across the network (e.g., firing a gun, opening a door). For that, we use RPCs.

Types of Unreal Engine RPCs:

1. **Multicast RPCs** – Function is called everywhere (used for effect like explosions).
2. **Server RPCs** – Function is called only on the server (used for gameplay functionality).
3. **Client RPCs** – Calls the function on one specific client only (for UI updates).

How to Implement a Server RPC (For Example Shooting a Gun):

1. Create a Shoot() function in PlayerCharacter Blueprint.
2. Mark it as **Run on Server** in function properties.
3. Insert shooting logic (spawn projectile, do damage).

Multiplayer Session Management (Creation, Find, and Joining)

Multiplayer games need a system through which players can find and join matches. Unreal Engine provides Sessions via the Online Subsystem.

Configuration of the Online Subsystem:

1. Run **DefaultEngine.ini** (in Config folder).
2. Add the following:
   - o [OnlineSubsystem]
   - o DefaultPlatformService=Null
   - o [OnlineSubsystemSteam]
   - o bEnabled=true
3. Reboot Unreal Engine.

Creating a Multiplayer Session (Blueprints):

1. Run GameInstance Blueprint.
2. Run CreateSession() function:
    o   Utilize Create Session Node.
    o   Add Number of Players.
    o   Add Public/Private status.

Finding and Joining Sessions:

1. Go to Main Menu UI Blueprint, and create Find Sessions function.
2. Utilize Find Sessions Node > Store Results.
3. Utilize **Join Session Node** when the player selects a game.

How to Use Unreal Engine's Advanced Networking Features

Network Relevancy (Optimizing Replication):

1. Replicate relevant actors to local players for improved performance.
2. Run **NetCullDistanceSquared** with greater values to replicate further.

Player Spawning & Team Selection:

1. Override **SpawnPlayer()** in **GameModeBase** to control where players spawn.
2. Utilize **Team-based spawning** for shooters or MOBAs.

Disconnects & Rejoining:

1. Apply **Seamless Travel** to enable players to rejoin when they disconnect.
2. Utilize **Save Game Data** to save player progress.

Multiplayer Game (Optimizing and Debugging)

Multiplayer games must be optimized well so that lag and sync do not happen.

Reducing Network Traffic:

1. Utilize **RepNotify** (Notify Clients Only When Data Changes)
2. Turn off Tick Replication on Non-Essential Actors
3. Utilize **Dormancy** (Pause Replication on Inactive Objects)

Debugging Network Issues:

1. Utilize **Net PktLag** command to add lag.
2. Activate **Network Profiler** analyze bandwidth usage.
3. Utilize **Stat Unit** to check server CPU/GPU functionality.

Testing Multiplayer Locally:

1. Navigate to Play Settings, choose "Number of Players = 2".
2. Open as **Standalone Game** to test network replication.

How to Install Dedicated Servers and Matchmaking

Dedicated servers provide you with more control over your game world, enhance the stability of the game and provide a smoother experience for users. Instead of the peer-to-peer connections, which are often the source of lag and connectivity issues, a dedicated server keeps everything centered. However, before you start, there are a few prerequisites that you'll need:

1. **Unreal Engine**: Make sure you have the latest version of Unreal Engine.
2. **A Dedicated Server Machine:** If you're hosting with a physical server or something like AWS or Digital Ocean, your server will need to be at the recommended spec for Unreal Engine.
3. **Understanding Networking**: At least a basic understanding of networking, including IP addresses and port forwarding, will be a big help.

Follow the steps below to install your dedicated servers:

Step 1: Setting Up Your Server

The first thing you're going to have to do is configure your server. If you have a physical box, update your OS. On cloud platforms, simply create a new instance that meets the demands. Also, make sure that your Unreal Engine server files are installed. They are needed to host the Unreal Engine server version.

Step 2: Installing Required Software

You will have to install software that facilitates networking and server management. For example, **SteamCMD** is one such that Unreal Engine developers use. Here's how you can install it as seen in the illustration below:

```
cd /path/to/your/directory
wget https://steamcdn-
a.akamaihd.net/client/installer/steamcmd_linux.tar.gz
mkdir steamcmd
mv steamcmd_linux.tar.gz steamcmd/
cd steamcmd
 tar -xvzf steamcmd_linux.tar.gz
```

This will download and install **SteamCMD,** which you will be using to manage game files and updates.

Step 3: Setting Up Your Game Project

After getting your server set up, now you get your game project ready. Launch your Unreal Engine project and navigate to settings. In the Project Settings, ensure you enabled the Dedicated Server build.

```
File > Package Project > Build Configuration > Development Server
```

Step 4: Running the Server

To boot your server, you will be required to use a command line approach. One easy command to begin with is seen in the illustration below:

```
cd /path/to/your/project/Binaries/Win64
YourGameServer.exe YourMap?listen -log
```

This command will start your dedicated server and enable logging output in case of any debugging you can do. Just replace **YourGameServer.exe** and **YourMap** with your game and map names, respectively.

Step 5: Firewall and Port Forwarding Setup

Now that your server is running, it's essential to configure your firewall settings. Ensure the necessary ports are open. Typically, Unreal Engine uses ports like 7777 for gameplay and 7788 for queries. Also, make sure to set up port forwarding on your router if you're using a home server. This way, external players can connect to your server.

Step 6: Testing Your Server

Get some friends to join your server. At this stage, testing functionality, gameplay, and experience is imperative. Find out any issues and squash them right away. You might need to adjust settings within the project or make server-side adjustments.

Multiplayer Game Security and Anti-Cheat Prevention

Multiplayer games built on Unreal Engine need robust security controls to prevent cheating, hacking, and exploits. Without any effective anti-cheat systems, a game is vulnerable to being tampered with, and the experience for genuine players is ruined.

Common Security Threats in Multiplayer Games

To start using security controls, you must become familiar with the most common cheats and exploits of online games:

Types of Cheats in Multiplayer Games:

1. **Aimbots & Wallhacks** – Cheating player aim or viewing through walls.

2. **Speed Hacks & Teleporting** – In-game speed or position modification to gain unfair rewards.

3. Memory Editing (Infinite Health, Ammo, etc.) – Modifying game memory to change variables.

4. **Packet Manipulation** – Interception and modification of packets from the internet (e.g., killing units involuntarily).

5. **DLL Injection & Code Modification** – Running a modification of game logic with additional code.

6. **Matchmaking Abuse & Fake Accounts** – Creating many accounts for spamming or crashing game servers.

Server vs. Client-Side Security:

1. **Client-Side Security** – Protects the player's game files from modification.

2. **Server-Side Security** – Protects against unauthorized game actions and network manipulation.

3. **Hybrid Approach** – Best security is with both client-side and server-side protection.

Setting Up a Secure Client-Server Architecture

Use a Dedicated Server (Avoid Listen Servers):

1. Dedicated Servers are more secure since they're not controlled by a player.

2. Listen Servers (Player-Hosted) can be exploited, since the host has direct access to server logic.

3. If hosting a Listen Server, utilize **Server Validation** for all important actions.

Always Validate Client Inputs:

Do not trust player input blindly and ensure to always validate movement, shooting, and damage on the server. For example:

1. Client sends movement request > Server validates it > Server applies movement.

2. Client fires bullet > Server validates if the player can shoot > Server logs damage.

How to Use Unreal Engine's Authority System for Anti-Cheat

Enforce Role-Based Authority (Server vs. Client Authority):

Server manages all important game data (player positions, damage, health, etc.).

Clients simply request actions and the server verifies them.

Replication & Secure Variables:

1. Utilize Replicated Variables with Server Control.

2. DO NOT allow client modification of important variables (Health, Ammo, Speed).

☑ Secure Example:

```cpp
UPROPERTY(Replicated, EditAnywhere, Category="Health")
float PlayerHealth;
```

⃠ Insecure Example:

```cpp
UPROPERTY(EditAnywhere, Category="Health")
float PlayerHealth;  // This is local to the client and can be hacked easily!
```

Preventing Memory Editing & Game File Hacking

Encrypt Game Data & Prevent Debugging:

1. Utilize **AES Encryption** for game data (scores, items, purchases) that is extremely sensitive.

2. Prevent Debugging Tools like Cheat Engine by adding this into DefaultEngine.ini:

    ```ini
    [SystemSettings]
    bAllowDebugViewmodes=False
    ```

3. Utilize Unreal Engine's **Pak File Encryption** to prevent extraction and modification of assets.

Detect & Prevent Memory Scanners:

1. Stop outside programs like Cheat Engine from changing in-memory values.
2. Utilize anti-memory scanning applications like BattleEye or Easy Anti-Cheat.

Protecting Player Movement & Physics Implementation

Server-Verified Movement:

1. Stop **Teleportation** and **Speed Hacks** by server-verification of player movement.
2. Utilize networked movement smoothing to eliminate lag issues.

```
void AMyCharacter::Server_MoveValidation_Implementation(FVector NewLocation)
{
    if (FVector::Dist(NewLocation, GetActorLocation()) < MaxAllowedDistancePerFrame)
    {
        SetActorLocation(NewLocation);
    }
    else
    {
        KickPlayer();
    }
}
```

How to Prevent Teleport Hacks:

1. Select movement timestamps to stop clients from teleporting.
2. Use **Server-Side Position Checking** to protect player positions.

Securing Combat, Damage, and Health Systems

Server-Side Hit Verification (Prevent Damage Hacks & Aimbots):

1. Prevent clients from calculating damage outcomes.
2. The server has to verify all hits through ray tracing or hitbox detection.

Anti-Cheat Tools & Detection Systems

Implementing BattleEye or Easy Anti-Cheat (EAC):

1. BattleEye and Easy Anti-Cheat detect hacks, injected DLLs, and aimbots.
2. Enable EAC Plugin in Unreal Engine:
   - Navigate to **Edit > Plugins**.
   - Turn on Easy Anti > Cheat.
   - Install it in Project Settings > Plugins > Easy Anti-Cheat.

Server-Side Cheat Detection Implementation:

1. Track suspicious activity, including:
   - Abnormally quick movement.
   - Abnormally precise headshots.
   - Players killing other players without viewing them.
2. Kick or Ban Cheaters Automatically:
   - Kick a player from the server if they exceed acceptable values.
   - Insert a simple ban system by IP or account ID.

Secure Multiplayer Sessions & Matchmaking

Prevent Fake Accounts & Matchmaking Abuse:

1. Ensure that online play account verification is compulsory (email, 2FA).
2. Implement server-side matchmaking verification to protect against ranked abuse.

Encrypt Network Packets (Prevent Packet Tampering):

1. Utilize **SSL encryption** for session and login data.
2. Prevent packet injection through validation of all client requests.

Server Performance & Network Security

Preventing DDoS Attacks:

1. Use **Cloud-Based DDoS Protection** (AWS Shield, Cloudflare, etc.).
2. Implement **Rate-Limiting** on login requests.

Secure Server Logs & Data:

1. Encrypt sensitive player statistics and progress data.

2. Save logs securely to observe suspicious player behavior.

Maintain Up-to-Date Security Measures

Cheaters evolve, so you need to ensure your security measures are fresh, follow the steps below:

1. Patch exploits & vulnerabilities once found.

2. Check game logs for hacking.

3. Stay in sync with Unreal Engine security patches.

Chapter 10

Cinematics & Virtual Production

How to Use Unreal Engine for Filmmaking and Cinematics

Filmmakers previously relied on pre-rendered CGI and expensive post-production pipelines, but with Unreal Engine, they can now have photo-realistic worlds, real-time lighting control, and interactive camera movements—all in a game engine.

Setting Up Your Filmmaking Project in Unreal Engine

Install Unreal Engine and Required Plugins:

1. Download and install Unreal Engine (UE5 recommended) from the **Epic Games Launcher**.

2. Enable the required plugins for filmmaking:

    o Sequencer (for editing the cinematic timeline).

    o Movie Render Queue (for rendering in high quality).

    o Virtual Camera (for real-time camera manipulation).

    o Live Link (for motion capture integration).

Set Up a New Cinematic Project:

1. Launch Unreal Engine and select **Film, Video & Live Events** as the project type.

2. Select a blank template to start from scratch or a **Virtual Production Template** in the case of LED walls and real-time tracking.

3. Put the **Scale Settings** on **Epic** for best visual quality.

Mastering the Sequencer:

Unreal Engine's Sequencer is the central filmmaking tool, allowing you to:

1. Animate cameras, characters, and objects.

2. Dynamically manipulate lighting.

3. Mix keyframe animations with real-time interactions smoothly.

If you want to Launch the Sequencer, follow the steps below:

1. Navigate Window > Cinematics > Sequencer.
2. Click **Add Level Sequence** to add a new cinematic sequence.
3. Add actors (characters, cameras, lights) to the Sequencer for animation.

Creating a Cinematic Scene in Unreal Engine

How to Import or Create an Environment:

To create an environment, follow the steps below:

1. Utilize **Quixel Megascans** for high-quality 3D assets.
2. Import models from Maya, Blender, or 3ds Max (FBX format).
3. Utilize **Unreal Marketplace** to search for pre-made environments.

To import assets, follow the steps below:

1. Navigate to Content Browser > Import.
2. Select your FBX, textures, or animation files.
3. Put the assets into the level and set them up like a film set.

How to Set Up Cinematic Lighting:

Realistic lighting adds to the visual quality of your movie. Follow the steps below:

1. Directional Light (for simulating sunlight)
2. Point Lights & Spotlights (for artificial light)
3. Rect Light (for soft studio light)
4. Sky Atmosphere & HDRI (for environmental light)

Note: Adjust light intensity, shadows, and color temperature to suit the mood of the scene.

How to Place and Animate Cameras:

1. Launch Sequencer and click +Track > Camera.
2. Pan the camera in the viewport (WASD to pan).
3. Apply **Cinematic Camera Actor** for film camera controls of the real world like focus distance, aperture, and depth of field.
4. Use **Keyframe** camera motion in Sequencer to achieve smooth camera movements.

Tip: Apply crane, dolly, and handheld presets to imitate real-world cinematography.

Character Animation and Motion Capture

Adding and Animating Characters:

1. Apply **MetaHumans** (from **Quixel Bridge**) for extremely realistic characters.

2. Import customized characters from Blender, Maya, or Mixamo.

To animate characters, follow the steps:

1. Use pre-built animations from the **Unreal Marketplace**.

2. Use Motion Capture with Live Link and Rokoko or Xsens suits.

Facial Animation and Lip Sync:

For realistic dialogue, follow the steps below:

1. Use **Live Link Face App** (iPhone-based facial tracking).

2. Use **MetaHuman Animator** for high-quality facial capture.

3. Use **AI-powered** voice synthesis (e.g., Replica Studios) for automatic lip sync.

Cinematic Effects and Post-Processing

How to Add Visual Effects (VFX):

1. Use **Niagara Particle System** for explosions, fire, smoke, and magic effects.

2. Use **Lens Flares & Bloom** for realistic cinematics.

3. Add **Motion Blur** and **Depth of Field** for enhanced film looks.

Post-Processing & Color Grading:

1. Add a Post-Process Volume to change:
   - Contrast & Saturation (for color grading).
   - Vignette & Film Grain (for cinematic look).
   - LUTs (Look-Up Tables) for pro color correction.

2. Use ACES Tone Mapping for Hollywood-style visuals.

Virtual Production Techniques

Using Green Screen & LED Walls:

1. Unreal's Compositing Tools allow real actors to be filmed against a green screen and composited with a 3D world.

2. LED Walls (e.g., The Mandalorian's Virtual Sets) project Unreal worlds in real-time behind actors.

Live Camera Tracking:

1. Use a real-world camera with Unreal Engine for virtual cinematography in real time.

2. Tracked Cameras (OptiTrack, Vive Trackers, ARKit Live Link) allow handheld-style shooting in virtual sets.

Final Cinematic Rendering and Export

Production-Quality Final Rendering using Movie Render Queue

For final output at production level, follow the steps below:

1. Launch **Movie Render Queue** (not regular Sequencer render).

2. Choose **Anti-Aliasing Settings** (8-16 samples per pixel for smooth edges).

3. Use **Path Tracing Renderer** (for Hollywood quality standard CGI).

4. Export frames as **EXR** sequences (for pro compositing in After Effects or Nuke).

Editing in External Software:

1. Import **EXR** frames in DaVinci Resolve, Adobe Premiere, or Final Cut Pro.

2. Finally, add sound design, grading, and final visual effects.

Advanced Cinematic Techniques With Unreal Engine

Virtual Reality Cinema Production (360° Cinematics):

1. 360-degree VR cinematic movie making is supported by Unreal Engine.

2. Use Omnidirectional Stereo Rendering for VR headsets.

AI-Controlled Cinematics & Procedural Animation:

1. Unreal Engine supports dynamically adjust framing based on character actions using camera automation powered by AI.

2. Unreal's Control Rig allows for procedural animation without keyframing.

Quick Tips to Making a Movie With Unreal Engine 5

To get started quickly with UE5 cinematography, have the following three things in mind.

1. **Add a Post-Process Volume**: Add a Post-Process Volume to your Level to activate an entire batch of filmmaker-friendly options.

2. **Motion Blur**: Under Post-Process Volume, you can switch on camera motion blur and achieve more natural, filmic-looking shots. Any movie ever projected in a movie theater traditionally will have motion blur due to the camera (film or digital).

3. **Depth of Field**: Use the **Depth of Field Film** feature in UE5 to add a nice focal point and bring one's attention to main objects in a shot. This will enable you to make scenes look more cinematic and realistic through the use of focus. There are many other options to try out as well, such as lens flares, grain, chromatic aberrations, etc.

4. **Enable Path Tracer**: Lastly, use the new path tracer to simulate realistic lighting in your scenes. The path tracer is one of the strongest tools UE5 has at its disposal, and it can be used to create stunning visuals with a photorealistic level of detail.

Virtual Production Workflows (LED Volumes, Real-Time Rendering)

Virtual Production (VP) changed the filmmaking process by combining real-time rendering with physical production techniques. With the help of LED volumes, real-time VFX, and motion tracking, directors can now film scenes in an enclosed environment and observe final VFX rendered in-camera.

Virtual Production combines computer graphics and live-action filmmaking to allow directors to:

1. Film actors in a virtual location projected onto LED screens.

2. Make adjustments to lighting, camera angles, and VFX.

3. Film final in-camera shots with reduced post-production work.

Key Technologies in Virtual Production:

1. **LED Volumes**: In real-time environments which are rendered within Unreal Engine, large LED walls are used for projection.

2. **Real-Time Rendering**: Leverages Unreal Engine's Nanite, Lumen, and RTX for rendering cinematic quality.

3. **Camera Tracking**: Syncs the real-world camera to Unreal's virtual camera to maintain perspective.

4. **In-Camera VFX (ICVFX)**: Overlays real-world actors and objects with digital environments in real time.

5. **Motion Capture (MoCap)**: Captures live actor performances and transfers them onto digital characters.

Benefits of Virtual Production:

1. **Cost Reduction**: Reduces on-location shooting expenses.

2. **Increased Turnaround**: Enables real-time iteration of lighting and settings.

3. **Authentic Lighting**: LED walls provide natural reflections and accurate light bounce off actors.

4. **Artistic Autonomy**: Directors can change locations instantly without re-shooting.

Installing a LED Volume for Virtual Production

Physical Composites of an LED Volume:

A typical LED volume setup comprises:

1. **Main LED Wall**: Displays the primary virtual scene.

2. **Side LED Panels**: Adds the scene to the sides of the main scene.

3. **LED Ceiling Panels**: Mimes natural top lighting and reflections.

4. **Tracked Camera**: Synchronize physical and virtual camera movement.

Unreal Engine Setup for LED Walls:

1. Install Unreal Engine (version UE5 preferred).

2. Enable Virtual Production Plugins: Navigate to Edit > Plugins and enable

   o nDisplay (for rendering to an LED wall).

   o Live Link (for camera tracking).

   o DMX (for lighting control).

   o Render Queue Movie (for high-quality rendering).

3. Make an nDisplay Configuration:

   o Navigate to Window > Virtual Production > nDisplay Config Editor.

   o Add new render nodes for each of the LED screens in the volume.

   o Set up the viewport, resolution, and tracking settings.

Integration of LED Screens to Unreal Engine:

1. Render multiple synchronized views on the LED walls using **nDisplay.**

2. Calibrate LED panels with Projection Mapping tools in Unreal.

3. Modify brightness, contrast, and color grading to mimic real-world lighting.

Creating Real-Time 3D Environments for LED Walls

Building Virtual Sets in Unreal Engine:

1. Use **Quixel Megascans** for high-definition photorealistic assets.

2. Import **Custom 3D Models** from Blender, Maya, or 3ds Max.

3. Optimize **Environments** with Unreal's Nanite (virtualized geometry) for real-time high-performance rendering.

Lighting for Real-Time Rendering:

1. Use **Lumen** (Global Illumination) to achieve dynamic, real-time lighting.

2. Add **HDRI Skybox** to mimic real-world lighting.

3. Adjust **Light Temperature** and **Intensity**, to mimic on-set lighting.

Virtual Camera and Parallax Adjustments:

1. Unreal Engine properly preserves parallax effects using camera tracking.

2. Move the virtual background with the camera to prevent perspective distortion.

Camera Tracking and In-Camera VFX (ICVFX)

Camera Tracking Setup:

To align the real camera with Unreal Engine, follow the steps below:

1. Use **Vicon, OptiTrack,** or **Vive Trackers** for tracking camera motion.

2. Connect the camera to **Live Link** in Unreal Engine.

3. Match the tracking settings to be fit with the size of the sensor and lens distortions of the actual camera.

In-Camera VFX (ICVFX) Workflow:

1. Real-time compositing allows the mixing of actors and props smoothly into the virtual set.

2. Modify **Focus, Depth of Field,** and **Exposure** for an absolute merge.

3. Apply Green Screen or Augmented LED Walls to add extra effects.

Live Production and Performance Capture

Motion Capture (MoCap) for Virtual Production:

1. Utilize Xsens, Rokoko, or Perception Neuron suits for full-body capture.

2. Add MoCap data to MetaHumans or Custom Characters in Unreal Engine.

3. Utilize **Live Link Face** (iPhone-based face tracking) for realistic facial animation.

Real-Time Directing and Adjustments:

1. Directors can make settings, lighting, and camera shot adjustments in real-time.

2. Use **Virtual Scouting** to see shots before shooting.

3. Dynamically change scene scaling, weather, and time of day.

High-Quality Rendering & Post-Production

Using the Movie Render Queue:

For the final render, use Unreal's Movie Render Queue:

1. Launch Movie Render Queue in Window > Cinematics.

2. Activate Anti-Aliasing (16x samples per pixel) for even edges.

3. Utilize **Path Tracing Renderer** for CGI film-quality rendering.

4. Render **EXR-format** frames for pro post-production in Nuke or After Effects.

Final Color Grading and Editing:

1. Import rendered clips into DaVinci Resolve or Adobe Premiere.

2. Do color correction and grading with **LUTs.**

3. Insert final VFX overlays, sound design, and CGI touches.

Chapter 11

Improvement & Performance Tuning

Performance Profiling Tools (Unreal Insights, GPU Profiler)

Performance profiling means analyzing your game's performance in order to figure out bottlenecks and also to optimize usage of resources. In Unreal Engine 5, this would entail monitoring several different factors such as frame rate, CPU use, memory consumption, etc.

Why Performance Profiling Matters:

Performance profiling is required to get your game to run decently on different hardware and other platforms. Jumpy performance results in horrible gameplay, thus lowering your game's success rate. During the performance profiling of the game, such things as listed below can be identified and subsequently resolved:

1. Low frame rate

2. Excessive use of CPU and/or GPU

3. Leaks in the memory

4. Lollygaging in loadings

Performance Profiling Tools Available in Unreal Engine 5:

Unreal Engine 5 comes with a set of tools that are designed to help you profile the performance of your game. Some of the most vital tools include:

1. **Unreal Insights:** A powerful profiling tool that provides you with high levels of performance detail.

2. **Console Commands**: Commands that you can use to monitor performance metrics in real-time.

3. **Profiler Window**: An in-game window that provides you with performance details and helps you identify bottlenecks.

How to Set Up Unreal Insights

Unreal Insights is among the best performance profiling assets available on Unreal Engine 5. Installing it requires that you to follow the steps below:

1. Launch your project inside Unreal Engine 5.

2. Proceed to the **Output Log** and input Insights.

3. Press **Enter** to activate the profiling session.

4. Play the game and run through the steps that you'd like to profile.

5. Close the profiling session upon completion by typing **Insights -Stop** inside the **Output Log**.

How to Analyze Performance Data

Once you've collected performance data using Unreal Insights, it's time to analyze it. Here are some key metrics to look at:

1. **Frame Rate:** Ensure your game has a consistent frame rate. Attempt to reach **60 FPS** or higher for a smooth game.

2. **CPU Usage**: Monitor CPU usage so that you can identify processes consuming excessive CPU.

3. **Memory Consumption**: Monitor memory usage so that you don't have memory leaks and can allocate memory more efficiently.

4. **GPU Usage:** Check GPU usage to ensure that your game is utilizing the GPU correctly.

Optimizing CPU Performance

CPU performance is important for maintaining a smooth frame rate. Some of these tips for CPU performance optimization include:

1. Reduce the draw call number by combining meshes and using instanced rendering.

2. Optimize your game logic in order to lower CPU overhead.

3. Use multi-threading to distribute workload on multiple CPU cores.

See the illustration below:

```cpp
// Example of multi-threading in Unreal Engine 5
void ExampleFunction()
{
 FRunnable* Thread = FRunnable::Create([]() {
 // Perform heavy calculations here
 }, TEXT("ExampleThread"));
 Thread->Start();
}
```

Optimizing GPU Performance

GPU performance is essential in rendering high-quality graphics. The following are some tips on how to enhance GPU performance:

1. Limit shaders and materials to keep GPU overhead low.

2. Optimize the rendering pipeline of your game to keep draw calls low.

3. Reduce GPU load wherever possible by using lower-resolution textures and models.

Optimizing Memory Usage

Memory usage can greatly influence the performance of your game. The following are some tips on how to enhance memory usage:

1. Profile your game's memory usage in order to track down memory leaks.

2. Use pooling techniques to recycle memory instead of creating new memory.

3. Optimize your game assets to reduce memory footprint.

Quick Tips and Tricks for Performance Profiling

Below are some tips and tricks to keep in mind while profiling your game's performance:

1. Profile frequently throughout the development process to detect problems early.

2. Test on multiple hardware configurations to ensure consistent performance.

3. Keep track of your profiling data to see progress and find areas for optimization.

Reducing Draw Calls and Optimizing Assets

Performance tuning for Unreal Engine helps in achieving high frame rates and smooth performance, especially for VR, open worlds, and cinematics. Having too many draw calls id often one of the biggest performance bottlenecks. Every object, material, and light effect can contribute to draw calls, which hold up the CPU and GPU. To find out how to reduce draw cells follow through in this section:

What are Draw Calls?

A draw call is a CPU request to the GPU to render an object. Each object, material, and shader add to the draw calls per frame. Large draw call numbers can result in:

1. CPU bottlenecks (the CPU is overwhelmed with rendering requests).

2. Frame rate drops (longer processing time per object).

3. Performance spikes when lots of objects are rendered at once.

How to Measure Draw Calls in Unreal Engine:

To track draw calls:

1. Launch the **console** (~) and enter:

    o stat RHI

    o Navigate to **DrawPrimitive** calls (ideal value: under 1000 for VR, under 2000 for standard games).

    o Alternatively, you can also use: **stat SceneRendering** to check rendering complexity.

Reducing Draw Calls in Unreal Engine

Using Static Mesh Instancing (Instanced Static Meshes - ISM):

Instanced Static Meshes (ISM) & Hierarchical Instanced Static Meshes (HISM) batch a number of instances of the same object together into a single draw call. Follow the steps below to enable ISM:

1. Build a Blueprint Actor.

2. Insert an Instanced Static Mesh Component.

3. Assign a mesh and create a duplicate.

4. Thereafter, Unreal Engine will group the objects as one draw call.

Merging Static Meshes to Minimize Draw Calls:

Instead of creating multiple individual objects, merge static meshes into large combined meshes.

Follow the steps below to merge meshes:

1. Choose multiple meshes in the viewport.

2. Navigate to Tools > Merge Actors.

3. Check Merge Static Meshes.

4. Use a single material (if possible) to reduce draw calls.

How to Reduce Material Draw Calls Using Material Instances:

Every material result in a new draw call. Instead of multiple duplicate materials, use Material Instances to have variations without additional draw calls. Follow the steps below to create Material Instances:

1. Right-click on an existing material.

2. Choose Create Material Instance.

3. Modify parameters like color, roughness, and metallic properties without producing additional draw calls.

Use Texture Atlases Instead of Separate Textures:

A texture atlas is a single large texture sheet that contains several textures. It reduces the number of texture lookups, thus increasing the rendering performance. Follow the steps below to create a Texture Atlas:

1. Merger several textures into a single large texture sheet in Photoshop or Substance Painter.

2. Assign UVs in a way to map objects onto the texture atlas.

3. Use a single material to put the atlas on multiple objects.

Minimizing Overdraw for Transparent Materials:

Transparent materials such as glass, smoke, and UI elements create excessive overdraw, which costs more to render. To reduce transparency follow the steps below:

1. Apply **Opaque Materials** in place of Translucent wherever possible.

2. In UI elements, apply **Masked materials** in place of Translucent.

3. Don't use large transparent surfaces (they take more passes to render).

4. Utilize **Dithered Opacity** in place of full transparency.

Asset Performance Optimization

Optimize Poly Count With LODs (Level of Detail Models):

High-poly models are expensive to render. LODs (Level of Detail) will automatically swap high-poly models with lower-poly models when an object is far away. Follow the steps below to enable LODs:

1. Launch a **Static Mesh** in the Content Browser

2. In the LOD Settings, click **Generate LODs**.

3. Modify **LOD** distances for balance between performance.

Using Nanite for High-Performance Meshes:

Nanite (Unreal Engine 5 feature) allows dynamic optimization of high-poly meshes, rendering the use of LODs obsolete. Follow the steps below to enable Nanite:

1. Launch a Static Mesh.

2. In the **Details** panel, enable **Nanite**.

3. Utilize **Automatic LOD** generation for further optimizations.

Optimize Texture Size and Format:

Large, high-resolution textures can cause memory bottlenecks. Unreal Engine includes support for compressed textures to optimize performance. Follow the optimization steps below:

1. Apply **2048 x 2048 (2K) or 1024 x 1024 (1K)** instead of 4K textures for small objects.
2. Utilize DXT1 (for solid) and DXT5 (for transparent) compression types.
3. Activate **Mipmaps** to reduce texture at distance.

Skeletal Mesh and Animation Optimization:

Skeletal Meshes (creatures, characters) are expensive because of bones and animation mixing. Apply the optimization methods below:

1. Remove unnecessary bones from skeletons.
2. Utilize animation compression (Right-click Animation > Apply Compression).
3. Turn off per-poly collision unless required.

Lighting Optimization for Performance

Reduce the Number of Dynamic Lights:

Dynamic lights are expensive to render as they require computation. Hence, follow the steps below:

1. Use **Static** or **Stationary Lights** in place of Movable Lights.
2. Reduce Shadow-Casting Lights.
3. Enable **Distance Field Shadows** for enhanced performance.

Use Baked Lighting (Lightmaps):

Baked lighting precomputes light and shadows, reducing real-time computation. Follow the steps below to bake lighting:

1. Put the lights to Static or Stationary.
2. Create lighting via **Build** > **Lighting Only**.
3. Change Lightmap Resolution in Mesh Settings.

Testing and Debugging Performance

Using Unreal Engine's Built-in Profilers:

To monitor draw calls and render performance, use:

1. **stat RHI** – Shows draw calls per frame.

2. **stat SceneRendering** – Checks render performance.

3. **r.ViewMode ShaderComplexity** – Confirms shader render performance issues.

Use GPU Profiler for Render Optimization:

1. Launch the console (~) and type:

   - stat GPU

2. Find high-spending rendering tasks.

3. Minimize shader complexity, dynamic shadows, and expensive materials.

Tips and Tricks for FPS Optimization on PC, Consoles and Mobile

FPS optimization in Unreal Engine is necessary in order to provide a smooth game experience on diverse platforms. PC, console, and mobile device performance optimization vary from each other based on the hardware, rendering techniques, and processing speed. Optimization methods for each platform are explained below

General Optimization Techniques (Applicable to All Platforms)

Profiling and Performance Analysis:

Analyze performance bottlenecks before optimizing using Unreal Engine's built-in tools:

1. Stat Commands (stat fps, stat unit, stat gpu, stat renderthread).

2. Unreal Insights for CPU/GPU profiling

3. GPU Visualizer (profilegpu) for locating expensive rendering operations

Minimizing Draw Calls:

1. **Merge Static Meshes**: Merges several meshes into a single draw call.

2. **Use Instanced Static Meshes**: Minimizes the draw calls for duplicate objects.

3. **Cull Unnecessary Objects**: Allow frustum culling, occlusion culling, and distance culling.

Level of Detail (LOD) Optimization:

1. Apply LOD models to meshes to reduce poly count at distant ranges.

2. Assign aggressive LOD switching on mobile to minimize triangle numbers.

Texture Optimization:

1. Apply **Texture Streaming** to load only visible textures.
2. Reduce texture resolution and use **Mipmaps.**
3. Compress textures with DXT (PC), ASTC (Mobile), and BC (Consoles) formats.

Lighting and Shadows:

1. Utilize **Baked** or **Static Lighting** in place of dynamic lighting when feasible.
2. Minimize Shadow Resolution and tune Cascaded Shadow Maps (CSM).
3. Use **Distance Field Shadows** for large environments.

Materials and Shaders:

1. Apply **Material Instances** instead of unique materials.
2. Optimize shaders by restricting instruction numbers.
3. Avoid expensive translucent materials, and use masked materials when necessary.

Post-Processing Optimization:

1. Turn off or minimize Bloom, Ambient Occlusion, Screen Space Reflections, Depth of Field, and Motion Blur.
2. Utilize **FXAA** instead of TAA or MSAA for anti-aliasing.
3. Scale down Chromatic Aberration and Lens Flare effects.

Optimization for Particle System:

1. Apply **GPU** particles instead of **CPU** particles.
2. Minimize the number of particles and update rate.
3. Apply **LOD** to particle systems.

Physics and Collision Optimization:

1. Utilizes basic collision shapes instead of advanced ones.
2. Do not use unnecessary rigid body physics simulations.
3. Minimize the number of real-time physics computations.

PC-Specific Optimization

Scalability Settings:

1. Allow users to modify settings like **shadows, effects, and view distance.**

2. Modify settings dynamically based on hardware detection.

GPU Optimization:

1. Activate NVIDIA DLSS, AMD FSR, or Intel XeSS for upscaling.
2. Optimize **Ray Tracing** by capping reflection samples and using Lumen efficiently.
3. Minimize high-poly assets by optimizing **Nanite meshes**.

CPU Optimization:

1. Apply multi-threading effectively by load-balancing CPU-bound tasks.
2. Optimize **AI Logic and Pathfinding** to minimize CPU overhead.

VRAM and Memory Management:

1. Optimize texture streaming pool size.
2. Minimize the quantity of high-resolution textures loaded at runtime.
3. Do not use redundant skeletal mesh influences.

Console-Specific Optimization (PS5, Xbox Series X, and Legacy Consoles)

Fixed Hardware Optimizations:

1. Optimize for fixed console hardware to prevent redundant dynamic scaling.
2. Utilize low-level APIs like DirectX 12 (Xbox) or GNM (PlayStation).

Memory Budgeting:

1. Follow strict memory budgets for textures, models, and audio
2. Compress assets down to available RAM.

Async Loading & Streaming:

1. Use background level streaming to avoid large load times.
2. Apply **HLOD (Hierarchical LOD)** for large worlds.

Frame Rate Targeting:

1. Lock at 60 FPS (or 30 FPS for stability on low-end hardware).
2. Apply **V-Sync and frame pacing** to avoid stuttering.

Mobile-Specific Optimization (Android & iOS)

Rendering Pipeline Optimization:

1. Apply **Forward Rendering** instead of Deferred Rendering.

2. Turn off Dynamic Shadows and use Baked Lighting.

Reducing Overdraw:

1. Do not use too many transparent materials and complex UI rendering.

2. Do not use decals and screen-space effects too much

Texture and Model Optimization:

1. Apply **512x512** or lower resolution textures.

2. Minimize **Poly Count** – ensure character models is under **10k-20k polygons**.

Shader Complexity Reduction:

1. Apply **Unlit Materials** when necessary.

2. Minimize **Normal Maps** and **Detail Maps** for better performance.

Mobile-Specific Rendering Settings:

1. Turn on **Mobile HDR** only where required.

2. Optimize **Instanced Static Meshes** for reducing draw calls.

3. Do not use expensive post-processing effects.

Physics and Collision Optimization:

1. Minimize the number of physics objects and real-time simulations.

2. Only utilize simple collision shapes.

Below is an Illustrative comparison of Platform-Specific Optimization:

Optimization	PC	Consoles	Mobile
Scalability Settings	Yes	No	Limited
Ray Tracing	Yes	Yes (Limited)	No
Texture Streaming	Yes	Yes	Yes (Low-Res)
AI Complexity	High	Medium	Low
LOD Usage	Yes	Yes	Aggressive
Physics Complexity	High	Medium	Low
Post-Processing	Medium	Medium	Low
Memory Budgeting	Medium	Strict	Very Strict

Chapter 12

Application of Unreal Engine for Non-Gaming Purposes

Architectural & Real Estate Use (ArchViz)

Architectural Visualization (ArchViz) is changing the way architects, designers, and real estate agents market projects. Unreal Engine provides photorealistic images, real-time interaction, and interactive virtual walkthroughs, making it the application of choice for modern architecture and real estate marketing.

Setting Up an ArchViz Project in Unreal Engine

How to Install & Set Up Unreal Engine for ArchViz:

1. Download Unreal Engine (UE5 is recommended) through the Epic Games Launcher.

2. Choose **Architectural Visualization Template** (or create a new blank project).

3. Go to the **Project Settings**, and activate:

   o Ray Tracing (realistic reflections and global illumination).

   o Lumen (Global Illumination & Reflections) for lighting.

   o Virtual Textures for enhanced material performance.

Importing 3D Models (CAD, Revit, SketchUp, Blender, 3ds Max):

Follow the steps below to insert an architectural model:

1. For 3ds Max, SketchUp, Blender - Export as **FBX or Datasmith**.

2. For AutoCAD & Revit > Import using **Datasmith Plugin**.

Follow the steps below to import:

1. Launch Content Browser > Import.

2. Choose your **FBX** or **Datasmith** file.

3. Select **Import Options** (optimize material settings and LODs).

4. Optimize hierarchy and arrange objects for better performance.

Optimizing the Scene for Performance

How to Minimize Polygon Count using LODs (Level of Detail):

1. Launch Static Mesh Editor.

2. Allow **Auto LOD Generation** to create optimized lower-poly versions of the assets.

3. Apply **Nanite** (UE5 feature) for detailed meshes with efficient rendering.

Material and Texture Optimization:

1. Apply **Material Instances** instead of making separate materials for each object.

2. Minimize the texture resolutions (2K instead of 4K wherever possible).

3. Apply **Virtual Texturing** on big surfaces (walls, floors).

Lightmap Optimization:

1. Before you import, first setup **UV Lightmaps in 3ds Max/Blender**.

2. Modify Lightmap Resolution in Unreal's Static Mesh Editor.

3. Apply **Baked Lighting** on static objects for improved performance.

Realistic Lighting for ArchViz

Choosing the Correct Lighting System:

1. Lumen (Recommended in UE5) – Dynamic global illumination & reflections.

2. Ray Tracing (High-End PCs) – Best for high-quality shadows & reflections.

3. Baked Lighting (Static Lightmaps) – Best for pre-rendered, performance-optimized scenes.

How to Setup Sunlight and Sky:

1. Insert **Directional Light** (Sunlight) and set intensity & angle.

2. Utilize **Sky Atmosphere** for realistic daylight.

3. Insert **Sky Light** (grabs ambient light from HDRI sky).

Interior Lighting Setup:

1. Utilize **Area Lights & Rect Lights** for natural window & interior lighting.

2. Insert **Point Lights** (lamp, spotlights, ceiling light).

3. Modify **temperature (Kelvin scale)** for warm or cold lighting.

Using High-Quality Materials and Textures

Applying PBR (Physically-Based Rendering) Materials:

1. The Unreal Engine has PBR materials, so it makes for realistic surface response to light.

2. Opt for photorealistic materials using **Quixel Megascans.**

3. Modify Normal Maps, Roughness, and Metallic values for depth and realism.

Using Parallax Occlusion for Detailed Surfaces:

For detailed floors, walls, and ceilings, using the following options:

1. Apply **Parallax Occlusion Mapping (POM)** instead of high-poly models.

2. Apply **Tessellation & Displacement** for additional depth on stone, brick, or wood surfaces.

Interactivity and Virtual Walkthroughs

Setting Up a First Person or Third Person Camera:

In order to set up a first-person or third-person camera, you need to consider the factors below:

1. **For Real Estate VR Tours**: Apply First-Person Character Controller.

2. **For Walkthroughs-Presentation Style**: Apply Cinematic Cameras with Path Animation.

Follow the steps below to set up a first person or third person camera:

1. Insert a Cine Camera Actor.

2. Launch Sequencer (Window > Cinematics > Sequencer).

3. Animate camera motion along a spline path for silky smooth tours.

How to Enable Material Customization:

1. Build a Blueprints for Dynamic Material Change.

2. Enable users to swap furniture, wall colors, and lighting options interactively.

3. Apply UI buttons (UMG – Unreal Motion Graphics) for easy selection.

How to Add Realistic Reflections and Glass Effects:

1. Apply Screen Space Reflections (SSR) or Ray Traced Reflections to mirrors & glass.

2. Apply **Opacity** and **Roughness** values to transparent objects.

Post-Processing & FX for Increased Realism

How to Use Post-Process Volume:

1. Insert a **Post-Process Volume** for cinematic tweaks.

2. Turn on Ambient Occlusion, Bloom, and Color Grading.

3. Apply **Exposure Settings** for realistic brightness transition.

How to Insert Atmospheric Effects:

1. Utilize **Volumetric Fog** for realistic light diffusion.
2. Insert Lens Flares and Bokeh Depth of Field for cinematic shots.

Exporting and Sharing the ArchViz Project

Rendering High-Quality Images and Videos:

1. Launch **Movie Render Queue** for high-quality cinematic exports.
2. Select **EXR format** for professional post-production in Photoshop or DaVinci Resolve.

Packaging for VR or Standalone Applications:

1. For VR: Turn on Oculus, Vive, or Windows Mixed Reality support.
2. **For Clients**: Set as a standalone application (File > Package Project).
3. **For Web**: Utilize **Pixel Streaming** to stream real-time walkthroughs over the internet.

Automotive Industry & Product Visualization

Unreal Engine is revolutionizing the automotive industry and product visualization with its rendering, photorealistic simulations, and interactive experiences. Car manufacturers, designers, and marketers use Unreal Engine to create virtual showrooms, configurators, driving simulations, and cinematic renders.

Preparing an Automotive Visualization Project

Installing Unreal Engine and Plugins:

1. Download Unreal Engine (UE5 is recommended) from the Epic Games Launcher.
2. Turn on the essential Plugins:
   - Datasmith (for CAD & 3D model import).
   - HDRI Backdrop (for authentic environment reflections).
   - Chaos Physics (for driving simulations).
   - Movie Render Queue (for high-quality renders).

How to Create a New Automotive Project:

1. Launch Unreal Engine.
2. Choose Automotive Visualization Template (or new blank project).

3. Modify Project Settings:

   o Enable **Ray Tracing** (for accurate reflections).

   o Set **Default RHI** to **DX12** for best performance.

   o Activate Lumen (for real-time global illumination).

Importing 3D Vehicle Models into Unreal Engine

How to Import CAD or 3D Models:

Below are the supported file types:

1. **Datasmith (.udatasmith)**: preferably used for CAD models from SolidWorks, CATIA, or Rhino.

2. **FBX (.fbx):** Suited for Blender, 3ds Max, or Maya models.

3. **OBJ (.obj)**: Suited for simple models without complex hierarchy.

Rendering High-Poly Car Models via Datasmith:

1. First, install **Datasmith Plugin** for 3ds Max, Rhino, or Revit.

2. Export the model as Datasmith (.udatasmith).

3. Navigate to **Content Browser > Import** and select the file.

Materials and Textures Optimization for Automotive Visualization

How to Create Photorealistic Car Paint Materials:

1. Launch Material Editor (Right-click > Create Material).

2. Utilize a PBR (Physically-Based Rendering) workflow:

   o Base Color: Modify metallic paint variations.

   o Metallic (1.0 for metal surfaces) and Roughness (varies for glossiness).

   o Normal Map for fine surface detail.

   o Clear Coat Layer (for realistic glossy car paint).

How to Use Material Instances for Color Customization:

1. Build a Material Instance (Right-click on Material > Create Material Instance).

2. Insert **Color Parameter Controls** (Scalar and Vector parameters in Material Editor).

3. Utilize **Blueprints** or **UI sliders** to allow users to dynamically adjust car color.

Adding High-Quality Glass and Metal Materials:

1. Glass: Utilize a Translucent Material with Reflection Capture for real glass.

2. **Chrome & Metal Parts:** Utilize a high metal value with reflection intensity.

Lighting Setup for Automotive Visualization

Using HDRI Backdrop for Natural Reflections:

1. Insert HDRI Backdrop (Add Actor > HDRI Backdrop).

2. Utilize **HDRI maps** via **Quixel Megascans or Polyhaven** for natural reflections.

3. Tweak/modify **Sky Light Intensity** based on scene brightness.

How to Set Up Studio Lighting for Car Renders:

For interior car showroom scene shots, follow the steps below:

1. Insert Rect Lights to simulate studio softboxes.

2. Utilize **Spotlights** to illuminate car edges.

3. Set up **Shadow Resolution** for high-definition contact shadows.

How to Enable Ray Tracing for High-Quality Shadows & Reflections:

1. Turn on **Ray Traced Reflections** for accurate car body reflection.

2. Utilize **Ray Traced Shadows** for smoother, more realistic shadow effects.

How to Add Interactivity to Car Visualization

How to Create a Car Configurator:

1. Utilize **Blueprints** to allow users to change car colors, wheels, and materials.

2. Create a UI using **Unreal Motion Graphics (UMG)** for basic customization.

3. Join **Material Parameters** to **UI buttons** for real-time adjustment.

Adding Camera Controls for Virtual Showrooms:

1. Utilize a **Cine Camera Actor** for cinematic shots.

2. Turn on Orbit Controls (Add Pawn > Spring Arm > Camera) for 360-degree perspectives.

Cinematic Animations for Automotive Marketing

Sequencer Setup for Cinematic Shots:

Follow the steps below:

1. Launch Sequencer (Window > Cinematics > Add Level Sequence).

2. Insert **Camera Tracks** and **Animate Movement** along a Spline Path.

3. Insert **Depth of Field & Motion Blur** for cinematic effects.

High-Quality Car Video Rendering:

1. Utilize **Movie Render Queue** for high-definition rendering.

2. Turn on **Temporal Anti-Aliasing** for smoother appearances.

3. Export in **EXR** format for post-processing in DaVinci Resolve or Premiere Pro.

Leveraging Driving Simulations in Unreal Engine

Setting Up Chaos Vehicle Physics:

Follow the steps below:

1. Activate Chaos Vehicle Plugin (Edit > Plugins > Chaos Vehicles).

2. Insert a Wheeled Vehicle Blueprint.

3. Modify **Suspension, Engine Torque,** and **Friction** for realistic driving physics.

Leverage AI for Traffic Simulation:

1. Insert **AI-driven** cars with the AI Navigation System on the Unreal Engine

2. Utilize **Spline Paths** to gain natural vehicle movement in traffic simulation.

Exporting and Sharing Automotive Visualizations

Deployment as a Standalone Application:

1. Deploy the project as a Windows, Mac, or VR package (**File > Package Project**).

2. Utilize **Pixel Streaming** for cloud-based car configurators.

VR and AR Support for Automotive Visualization:

Follow the steps below:

1. Insert Oculus, HTC Vive, or Varjo XR support for VR car showrooms.

2. Utilize **ARKit & ARCore** for virtual car placement in real-world environments.

Medical Simulations & Training Programs

Unreal Engine provides an extensive framework to create high-fidelity medical simulations for improved skill acquisition and procedure precision.

Medical simulations in Unreal Engine can be categorized into the following types:

- **Surgical Training Simulations**: Simulation of complicated surgeries.
- **Patient Interaction Simulations:** Training in diagnosis and communication.
- **Triage/Emergency Simulations**: Practice of life-critical situations like CPR.
- **Anatomy and Physiology Practice**: Interactive study units for students.

Setting Up the Development Environment

Step 1: Install Unreal Engine

- Download and install Unreal Engine through the Epic Games Launcher.
- Enable Blueprint and C++ for added flexibility.
- Install required plugins (Niagara for particle effects, Chaos Physics, VR integration tools).

Step 2: Choose Rendering Options

- High-fidelity graphics (Nanite & Lumen) for PC/VR sims.
- Optimized Mobile/AR configuration for less-powered devices.

Step 3: Install Required Plugins

- Launch **XR & VR Expansion Plugin** for virtual reality simulations.
- Use **Live Link Face** for live facial motion capture in patient interaction training
- Add **Metahuman Creator** for realistic character models.

How to Create a Medical Simulation

Step 1: Creating the Virtual Environment

- Utilize **Quixel Megascans** for realistic hospital environments.
- Optimize lighting and reflections for maximum realism without performance overhead.
- Apply physics-based interactions (pick-up of tools, managing patients).

Step 2: Developing Interactive Medical Equipment

- Utilize **Blueprints** to create interactive objects like surgical instruments.

- Activate haptic feedback for VR controllers.
- Activate real-time physics simulation for medical procedures.

Step 3: Realistic Human Anatomy Implementation

- Utilize 3D models of organs, bones, and tissues.
- Add body functions like heartbeat, breathing animations.
- Utilize procedural slicing for surgical simulations.

Step 4: AI-Driven Patient Behavior

- Apply AI-driven patients with varied reactions.
- Utilize behavior trees for dynamic response to medical procedures.
- Utilize voice recognition & response for diagnosis training.

How to Enhance Realism With Advanced Features

The features include:

1. Haptics & Force Feedback:
   - Add haptic gloves or VR controllers for force feedback.
   - Make use of haptic suits in high-end simulation training.
2. Multiplayer & Online Collaboration:
   - Insert multiplayer networking in team simulation.
   - Utilize dedicated servers or peer networks for remote learning.
3. AR & Mixed Reality in Training:
   - Design mobile AR training apps.
   - Install Microsoft HoloLens integration to support mixed reality training.

Factors to Consider for Optimization & Performance

They include the following:

1. Graphics Optimization:
   - Utilize Level of Detail (LOD) models to reduce poly count.
   - Optimize materials and textures for performance.
2. Physics & Collision Optimization:
   - Utilize simplified collision meshes on objects.

- o Reduce real-time physics calculations to enable a smoother performance.
  3. Mobile & VR Performance Optimization:
     - o Activate Mobile Forward Rendering for AR/VR.
     - o Minimize shader complexity & overdraw.
     - o Apply precomputed lighting instead of dynamic lighting.

Deployment & Testing

Testing & Debugging:

Follow the steps below:

1. Utilize Unreal Insights & Profilers to monitor performance.
2. Carryout user testing with medical professionals for feedback.

Deployment to Multiple Platforms:

1. For PC (Windows, macOS)
2. For VR (Oculus, Vive, HoloLens)
3. For Mobile (iOS, Android) package

VR/AR for Education & Industrial Applications

Real-time rendering, physics simulation, and support for VR/AR by Unreal Engine provide high-fidelity simulations for education, skill acquisition, and industrial procedures.

Advantages of VR/AR in Education:

1. **Immersive Learning**: Topics are learned by students in 3D space, improving engagement.
2. **Safe Environments**: Simulations and virtual labs replace real life dangers.
3. **Interactive Content**: Allows for hands-on learning through interactive models.

Based on the advantages outlined above, the following are the examples of VR/AR in Education:

1. **Medical Training**: Virtual reality surgery simulation.
2. **STEM Education**: Chemistry, physics, and engineering experiments in virtual reality.
3. **History & Geography**: Virtual field trips to historical sites.

Advantages of VR/AR in Industrial Training:

1. **Workforce Training**: Employees practice tasks before real-world environments.
2. **Reduces Errors:** Training simulated to prevent costly real-world mistakes.
3. **Remote Collaboration:** AR overlays and VR remote assistance increase productivity.

Based on the advantages outlined above, the following are the examples of VR/AR in Industrial Training:

1. **Manufacturing:** Virtual reality-based assembly line training.
2. **Aviation & Automotive**: Aircraft and vehicle engine simulations.
3. **Construction & Architecture**: AR-supported building inspections.

How to Create a VR/AR Project in Unreal Engine

Setting Up Unreal Engine & Plugins:

1. Download and install Unreal Engine (UE5 recommended) via the Epic Games Launcher.
2. Activate the required VR/AR Plugins (Edit > Plugins):
    o OculusVR, SteamVR, OpenXR (for VR headsets).
    o ARKit (iOS), ARCore (Android) (for mobile AR).
    o Live Link XR (for live motion tracking).

How to Create a New VR or AR Project:

For VR, follow the steps:

1. Select **Virtual Reality Template** when creating a new project.
2. Apply the **First-Person Pawn** for interactive experiences.

For AR, follow the steps below:

1. Choose **Handheld AR Template** for mobile augmented reality applications.
2. Apply **AR Pawn with AR Session** for plane detection and object placement.
3. Enable Project Settings for VR Performance (Edit > Project Settings).
    o Set **Frame Rate** to **90-120 FPS** for VR (prevents motion sickness).
    o Activate **Forward Rendering** for better VR performance.
    o Optimize with **Fixed Foveated Rendering** for mobile VR (Oculus Quest).

Creating Interactive VR/AR Environments

Importing 3D Models and Environments:

1. Import **CAD models (Datasmith)** for industrial simulations.
2. Utilize **Quixel Megascans** for realistic textures in education apps.
3. Design **Blueprint Actors** to introduce interactivity into objects.

Setting Up a VR Player (Motion Controllers & Interaction):

1. Insert a VR Pawn (Create a new Blueprint > VRPawn).
2. Mount **VR Camera & Motion Controllers** to track player's head and hands.
3. Provide **Hand Interaction** (Grab, Point, Press Buttons) with:
   o Physics Handle Component (to grab objects).
   o Widget Interaction Component (to interact with UI in VR).

Setting Up an AR Player (Object Placement & Interaction):

1. Utilize **AR Session Component** to enable plane detection.
2. Insert **AR Pin Component** to pin virtual objects to real-world space.
3. Use **AR Line Trace** to identify surfaces and allow users to position objects.

Inserting Physics & Simulations for Realistic Training

How to Use Chaos Physics for VR-Based Industrial Training:

1. Activate Chaos Physics Engine (Edit > Plugins > Chaos).
2. Insert Rigid Body Physics to objects (Turn on Simulate Physics in Object Properties).
3. Add **Constraints & Joints** for realistic machine assembly simulations.

Real-Time Damage & Material Deformation Implementation:

1. Add **Destructible Meshes** to create breakage of objects simulation.
2. Utilize **Dynamic Material Changes** for stress and temperature simulation.

AI & Multiplayer Integration for Collaborative Training

AI-Driven VR Training Assistants:

1. Apply **Behavior Trees (AI > Behavior Tree)** to create AI instructors in VR.
2. Script voice feedback & real-time guidance for users.

Enabling Multiplayer Support for Remote VR/AR Training:

1. Utilize the **Unreal Engine Multiplayer Framework** for shared collaboration.
2. Add **Pixel Streaming** to enable remote VR/AR training over the web.

Creating UI & Feedback Systems for VR/AR Applications

How to Insert In-VR UI with Unreal Motion Graphics (UMG):

1. Install 3D Widgets (Add Widget Component to VRPawn).
2. Assign **UI** features to motion controller interactions.

Applying Haptic Feedback to VR Training:

1. Utilize **Haptic Feedback Component** to simulate touch reactions.
2. Enable haptic reactions which activates when users click virtual objects.

Optimizing VR/AR Performance for Smooth Experience

Reducing Draw Calls for VR Performance:

1. Apply **Instanced Static Meshes (ISM)** for repeated objects.
2. Activate **Occlusion Culling** to occlude off-screen objects.

Optimizing AR for Smartphones:

1. Utilize **Lightweight Materials** (avoid real-time reflections).
2. Minimize Polygon Count with LODs (Level of Detail).

Deploying & Publishing VR/AR Apps

Setting Up VR Apps for Headsets:

1. For Oculus/Quest: Turn on OculusVR Plugin and set as APK.
2. **For SteamVR**: Utilize **OpenXR Plugin** for PC VR publishing.

Setting Up AR Apps for iOS & Android:

1. For iOS: Turn on ARKit Plugin and set as as.ipa.
2. For Android: Turn on ARCore Plugin and set as.apk.

Conclusion

In conclusion, Unreal Engine 2025 represents a monumental leap in both gaming and non-gaming applications, showcasing a versatile toolkit that empowers creators across industries. From its groundbreaking features like Nanite virtualized geometry and Lumen global illumination to its real-time rendering capabilities, Unreal Engine continues to redefine what is possible in terms of visual fidelity and interactivity. The integration of advanced systems such as Metasounds for immersive audio and Niagara VFX for stunning visuals further elevates the engine's performance, ensuring that users have the tools necessary to create top-tier experiences in gaming, film, architecture, and beyond.

In this book, we have discussed the essential elements of Unreal Engine 2025, guiding you through everything from setting up the engine and understanding its architecture to mastering the workflows for game development, cinematics, and virtual production. We also looked into advanced topics like AI and machine learning, multiplayer development, and VR/AR, each of which is pushing the boundaries of innovation in their respective fields.

Furthermore, we have examined how Unreal Engine is not just limited to game development but has expanded into industries such as automotive visualization, medical simulations, and educational applications. This flexibility underscores the engine's importance as a cutting-edge tool that is reshaping the way professionals approach digital content creation.

As you continue your journey with Unreal Engine 2025, remember that it is more than just a tool; it is a catalyst for creativity, pushing the envelope on what can be achieved in virtual worlds. Whether you are an aspiring game developer, a filmmaker, a virtual architect, or a researcher, Unreal Engine 2025 is your gateway to turning visionary ideas into reality.